A High School English Teacher's Guide to Writing Memoir

A High School English Teacher's Guide to Writing Memoir

Coley Conter, Mary Ehrenworth, and Lauren Gould

Routledge
Taylor & Francis Group
NEW YORK AND LONDON

A Stenhouse Book

Designed cover image: Illustrations by Lauren Gould

First published 2026
by Routledge
605 Third Avenue, New York, NY 10158

and by Routledge
4 Park Square, Milton Park, Abingdon, Oxon, OX14 4RN

Routledge is an imprint of the Taylor & Francis Group, an informa business

Interior illustrations by Lauren Gould

ISBN: 978-1-032-98875-7 (pbk)
ISBN: 978-1-003-60657-4 (ebk)

DOI: 10.4324/9781003606574

Typeset in Sabon LT Pro
by KnowledgeWorks Global Ltd.

Dedications

From Coley:
To Meem, for teaching me to never turn my back on the ocean.

From Mary:
To Jenny Killion, who inspired high school writers to tell their stories with grace and power, and whose friendship has meant the world to me.

From Lauren:
To Mom, who surrounded me with stories and taught me how to tell my own.

Contents

Dear Colleagues,

Please consider this an invitation to adapt, expand, and experiment with these lessons to fulfill your desires, meet the needs of your students, *and* help them unlock their potential. We hope to save you some planning time, expand your resources, help you achieve your vision … and inspire you to consider new frontiers.

We have many resources, from charts and tools to mentor texts and student exemplars, available at hs-guidetoteaching.org. You may reach us there as well connect and share what you've been trying.

We can't wait to see where you take these lessons (and your students' writing)!

All the best,

Coley, Mary, Lauren

Introduction: Why Write Memoir

In a memoir, feelings are more important than facts,
and to write honestly, I have to confront my demons.
—Isabel Allende

As Isabel Allende remarks, memoir is an invitation to revelatory honesty. We adore memoir for how it helps young writers hold onto beauty and write through trouble. Adolescence is hard. It's the time of your life when you have the least power and the most anxiety. Teens are gorgeous memoir writers, because their lives are cauldrons of anxiety and pressure and emotion. Mary Karr describes the aptness of memoir as the genre for worriers and sufferings, saying: "Part of what murders me about memoir—what I adore—is its democratic (some say ghetto-ass primitive), anybody-who's-lived-can-write-one aspect" (2016, xiii). Stephen King is a little more cautious, but ultimately optimistic about all humans as storytellers, saying: "I believe large numbers of people have at least some talent as writers and storytellers, and that those talents can be strengthened and sharpened" (2010, 18).

Teens' talents *can* be strengthened and sharpened. *And* their raw storytelling is potent. Because they exist in crucibles of angst, and because trouble is the friend of a writer, memoir is a good genre for teens. Lisa Damour (2019), author of *Under Pressure*, describes the combustible pressures that teenagers deal with, especially in this age of social media, where every decision, every invitation, every incident can be documented and shared.

Writing is a way to handle stress, a way to think about it, and a way to move forward. Writing lets teens think about their relationships, about the urgent social issues that shape their lives, and about what preoccupies them. It also helps them hold onto those mundane, quirky moments of beauty that bring us joy. Katherine Bomer writes of memoir, "We want to understand what our lives mean. And we want someone else to witness what life was like for us because it helps us feel real. Writing an autobiography or memoir helps satisfy those longings and brings clarity to the events and relationships that haunt us" (2005, xiii). In *Narrative Writing with Latinx Teens: Testimonios, Texts, and Teaching,* Carla España shares her field notes and her insights from inviting Latinx teens to tell their stories. She begins with a vignette of a sixth grader saying that the impetus for her story was the need to *desahogarme.* Carla presents *desahogarme* as a metaphor, which she describes as the way writers use writing "to get something off their chest, to vent, to release something huge that is bottled up" (2024, xvii).

We often see this process of unbottling occur in memoir units. We see teens struggle, at first, to decide to share their stories, and then enjoy the incredible beauty when they do. In an interview with *Education Week*, Gholdy Muhammad, author of *Unearthing Joy: A Guide to Culturally and Historically Responsive Teaching and Learning* (2023) described joy as, in part, "teaching our children to name the beauty within themselves and humanity" (Ferlazzo 2023). Not all parts of the curriculum help children find and name the beauty in themselves, but memoir is our partner in this work.

Your students will ask, and you may worry, about the role of truth inside of memoir. Most writers note that memoirists won't remember every detail, which gives them permission to craft a story they want to tell. Mary Karr says, "There's artifice to the relationship between any writer and her reader. Memoir done right is an art, a made thing. It's not just raw reportage flung splat on the page." (2016, xvii). Your students aren't jotting diary entries. They are recreating a moment, a scene, a feeling. As they do so, give them permission to play, with language, with structure, with register. Felicia Rose Chavez (2021) comments on how most of the time, students write for teachers, reaching only toward a task, a rubric, a grade, all of which reflect someone else's vision of writing. Memoir is a moment when your students can write with more freedom, more intimacy.

And we also know that every job interview, every college and scholarship application starts with "Tell me about yourself." Storytelling is essential to how we make friends, how we launch relationships, and how we form our beliefs about ourselves and the world. Learning to tell your own story with purpose and confidence is a beautiful gift we can give students.

You'll find, as well, that you get to know your students in a completely different way when you teach memoir. Every day, you come in, and you listen to young people tell you their stories, and you help them craft those stories to reveal their meaning. It's beautiful. And it's important. In *Culturally Responsive Teaching and the Brain,* Zaretta Hammond (2015) notes how all of us, as teachers, inevitably build rapport unconsciously with certain types of students. Perhaps you are drawn to the quiet introverts, or to the readers. Perhaps you love the naughty ones, or the troubled ones. All of us see some students more easily and quickly than we do others. Memoir helps us see all of our students.

Mapping Your Curriculum

This guide offers more than forty flexible lessons, giving you plenty of choice as you plan your memoir unit. You might select a few favorite lessons to enhance your existing unit or use this resource as a foundation, picking several lessons from each chapter to create an entirely new unit. These lessons are not intended to be taught in a strict sequence; instead, they're intentionally designed to honor your agency as a teacher and make the art (and work) of planning a little lighter.

Most lessons in this guide follow a minilesson structure: a short, focused teaching point followed by immediate student practice. Lessons typically begin with a quick demonstration or model, transition into guided practice, and then move students toward independent work.

Keeping instruction brief and targeted maximizes student engagement, helps them retain key skills, and provides ample time for authentic writing practice. Lessons help students build momentum and confidence as writers, allowing them to quickly apply new strategies into their own writing.

The chapters in this book are set up so that you can make choices—choices about how long your memoir unit will be and choices about which lessons you might teach as *whole-class lessons* and which you might convert into *micro lessons*, *small groups*, or *stations*. Converting lessons into shorter formats allows you to condense your unit when you are pressed for time and support students with differentiated instruction.

- *Whole-class lessons* introduce or remind students of a strategy that will make them more powerful. We reserve whole-class lessons for strategies we're sure will benefit all, or almost all, of our writers, though during work time, students may not always be practicing only this strategy.
- *Micro lessons* make for fast-paced, guided practice. When we think of micro lessons, we picture a single period where we might teach a short lesson, give students a chance to try it, teach another, give them a chance to try that, and so on.
- *Small groups* allow for targeted instruction you are giving only to a few students, while others are working.
- *Stations* are a kind of midway point between these, where you set up workspaces around the room where students can choose to study and try certain writing techniques. To convert any of these lessons into stations you can either a) invite students to read the lesson and play the role of both teacher and student or b) convert the lesson into a short handout with steps.

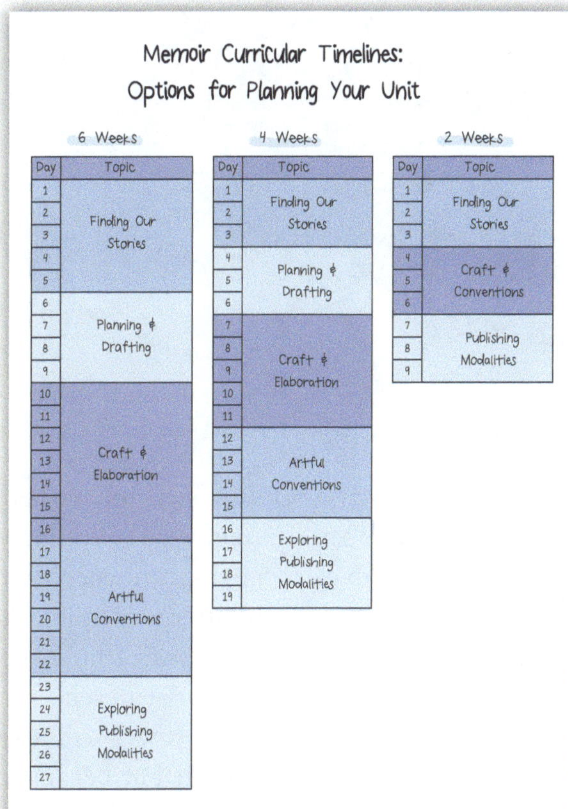

You'll make different choices about how many of these lessons you'll teach, depending first on whether you are using these lessons as a curriculum or if you are inserting them into your existing unit, and second, how many days and weeks you have to teach memoir. On our website (hs-guidetoteaching.org), we share some detailed calendars for planning memoir using these lessons, depending on if you have two weeks, four weeks, or seven weeks. You may find these more detailed plans helpful as you plan your own curriculum.

Teaching and Coaching Inside a Workshop Structure

Teaching inside a workshop structure allows you to demonstrate a strategy or launch an inquiry and then set up students to write for the rest of the period, during which time you can confer with writers or teach small groups. There is never enough time for either of the latter in secondary schedules, and so you'll see we've made some suggestions for days when you don't teach a lesson and instead teach micro lessons or small groups. It's also fine to have a day when you don't teach a lesson at all, and your kids work on their writing while you confer. Those kinds of days work best after you've done some mentor text work or taught a few lessons that writers can capitalize on, so students have enough to do.

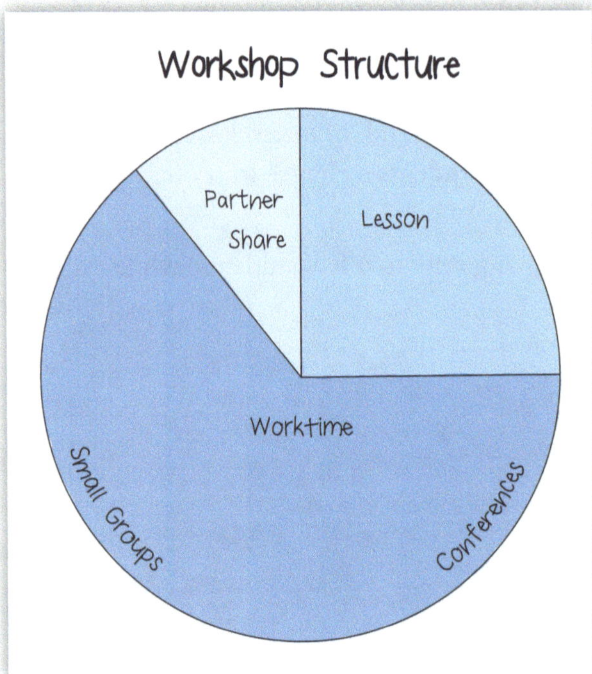

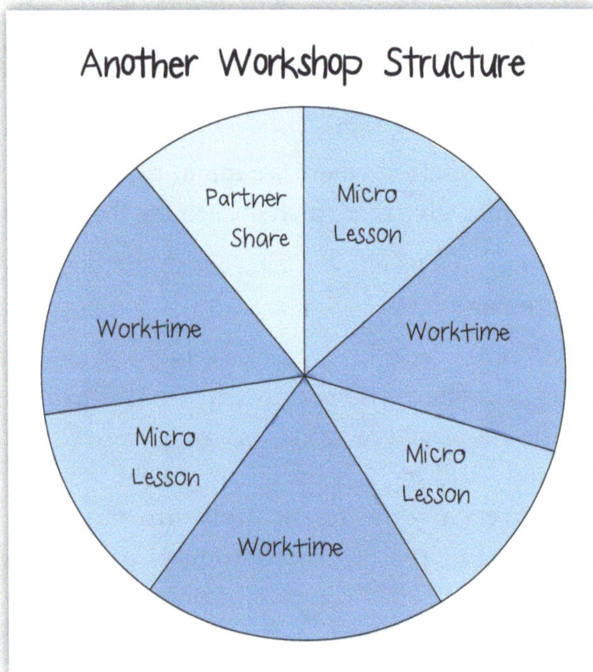

Independent Work Time

One of the goals of workshop structure (where you demonstrate or lead an inquiry, then kids have time to work on their writing, usually ending with a partner share) is for kids to have time to work on their writing in class, in your presence. With AI becoming so accessible as a writing coach, and if kids are unwise, a pinch-hitter writer, it's all the more important for kids to do some drafting in your presence, so you get an idea of how they write on their own. It's also more democratic for all kids to have some time to write in school, where you know they have a quiet environment that is relatively free of distractions (there will also be young writers who write much better outside of school, not because they use AI but because they escape the tumultuous social pressures of high school classrooms).

When we are in a writing unit—spending several days working on writing—we give kids time to write in class, so they build some energy for their writing, and so we can observe and talk to them while they are in the midst of writing.

Conferring and Coaching

Another goal of workshop structure is that while writers work, you carve out time to talk to kids about their writing. We tend to structure that time in two ways. Sometimes we confer—we pull up alongside one writer, or a partnership, and we talk to them about their work, listening, giving advice, offering tools. Other times, we plan small groups, either as seminars that any writer can join, or as targeted instruction to support certain writers. In *Write Beside Them* (2008), master teacher Penny Kittle described her sense of joy when she knew she would be teaching writing—that her day would be spent listening to and talking to kids about their writing. Writing workshop is structured to help you have more time to achieve that kind of intimacy.

You'll find, inside each lesson, prompts for conferring, ones that we think will help you coach individual writers or partnerships. They reflect our experience with the predictable ways that some students might benefit from a little support, while others may be ready to extend the work of the lesson. For example, here you see suggestions for supporting kids once you've taught a lesson for multilingual learners on crafting compelling dialogue:

Prompts to Coach Students and Partnerships:

- *Sometimes you realize that you already have a lot of dialogue, and then the question you can ask yourself is: Where can my dialogue be more powerful?*
- *If you don't have any dialogue in your story, ask yourself if dialogue might help develop the perspective of other characters.*
- *Adding tone of voice and body language has a surprising effect—it often adds to tension in a story. You can think about how it either can contrast or reinforce what is said.*

Charts and Tools

This book is full of charts, all available for download on our website. Grant Wiggins, who published many articles and books about the challenges of transfer, often referred to charts and tools as cueing systems for transfer (Wiggins and McTighe 2008, 2024). Kids need reminders of their learning that they can refer to as they work.

The charts and tools included here are intended for you to share with students, post, remake alongside students during lessons, or use during conferences and small groups. If you share them with kids, feel free to pass them off as yours. If you share them with colleagues, we'd appreciate it if you'd reference this book, and perhaps Lauren as chart-maker—although we collaborated on content, Lauren is the artist who created these jewels.

One of the things we love about elementary classrooms (besides the beautiful bulletin boards and robust classroom libraries) are the writing centers that kids can freely use. They house charts and sticky notes and pens and mentor texts for writers to grab as they brainstorm, draft, and revise. Because elementary teachers don't share a room, they can create robust writing environments. Chances are you do share a room, or you move around, or you work from a cart. We've taught in all of those modes and it is … annoying. Still, look at the classrooms where you do teach, and consider setting up a portable writing center in those classrooms, knowing that kids can then grab charts and tools and supplies as needed. Or you might upload these charts to a Padlet or other digital site, as a reference for your students.

Setting Up Writing Partnerships

In this, of all genres, it's important to get students into stable writing partnerships. Teens are going to do braver, better work in the company of peers whom they trust. Tyrone Howard et al. often calls these partnerships *learning alliances*, which captures the sense of students as interdependent beings, joined in a learning coalition (2020). In general, we love our students to have some voice over their partnerships, while we also do some social engineering. You can't go wrong by beginning with kids partnering with whoever they sit next to—kids rarely sit next to someone they are afraid of or dislike. Then you can study these partnerships and adjust them so they are supportive and productive. Sara Ahmed, author of *Being the Change,* calls this process "kid watching," and it's a way to study kids' full selves and use that knowledge to deepen relationships.

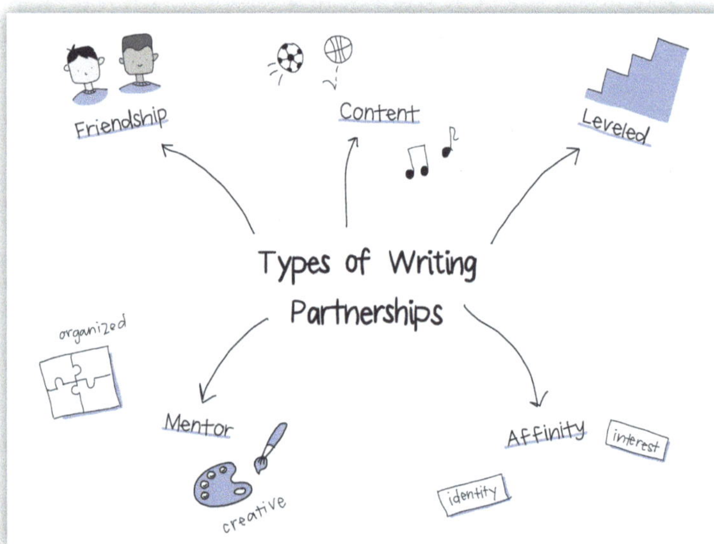

We often organize kids into different kinds of partnerships (all of which can be operating in the same class). You might, for example, have many of your students in *friendship* partnerships, since in this genre, especially, risk-taking is more important than writing proficiency. You might have some students in *content* partnerships (students who are writing about loss, for instance). Sometimes *leveled* partnerships are helpful—often fast, proficient writers enjoy being partnered, and you can give them special mentors and coaching, for example. Occasionally *mentor* partnerships can be helpful, where one partner is an organizational mentor, keeping track of what's due, or one partner is a language mentor, helping with translations, and so on. And sometimes you may have some students who would like to be in an *affinity* partnership, pairing up with someone who shares part of their identity.

The main thing is that once writers begin to share their stories with a partner, they should talk to that same partner across the writing process. Memoir is a courageous business, best tackled in the company of those we feel safe with.

Your Role as a Mentor Writer

Your role as a mentor writer will matter—it will engage and inspire your young writers. For the stories you tell, you'll want to excavate your teenage years, digging up stories from middle and high school. Remember, the goal of sharing your stories is to inspire your students in finding their stories. You also, with every risk you take as a writer, stir up teens to be brave. Think about the issues you struggled with as a teen, the relationships that were challenging, the stereotypes and norms that haunted you, and you'll find, pretty quickly, that you have a lot to write about too. As you share your stories with your students, remember to add reflections, such as, "When I think about this now, I think this moment was really about ... jealousy or competition or fitting in." Your students won't have the same moment to tell as you did, but they will have plenty of stories about the same issues so many adolescents experience.

Your students would love to hear your stories, and your stories deserve to be told. Sometimes, however, we are pressed as teachers and would prefer to borrow someone's demonstration text. You can, of course, share any of the stories that we share here of our childhoods. Simply say, "One of my friends, Coley, wrote," or "One of my colleagues, Mary, told this story," or "A writer I know, Lauren," for example. Borrow away—everything we wrote here, we wrote for you and your students, in the hope that our storytelling will be generative for yours.

When you show your writing to students, you have a few choices. You could show a small chunk of it while explaining your process as a writer. You could lead an inquiry and invite students to notice and name the moves and decisions you made as a writer. Above all, it's best to write in front of students in real time. This doesn't necessarily mean you have to "wing" it. Often, we know what we're going to write, or how we're going to revise, but we model that thinking in real time in front of students. Writing in front of your students allows them to see you grapple with the same process they will encounter. Sometimes when we show young writers only our polished pieces, the writing can seem unattainable. You can also invite kids to write along with you, asking them to try out what the dialogue in this part might sound like or asking them to brainstorm a few words to help build the mood of a dreadful walk home.

Inculcating Writing Process and Mentor Text Immersion

One of the most important aspects of this work is that your writers internalize a writing process that they can bring to every task and every genre. Ultimately, because they have you as a writing teacher, your students will be confident tackling any writing task, knowing that they will spend a little time on each stage: researching/collecting, planning and drafting, revising/raising the level, and publishing. In these two visuals, you can see a flowchart of the writing process overall and one writer's personal writing process.

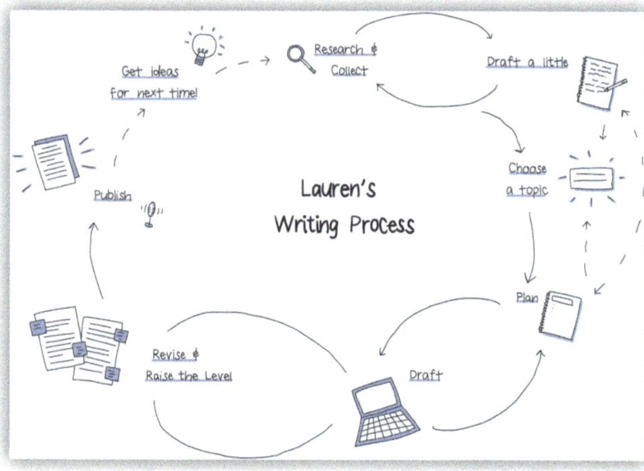

We want students to grow familiar with the components of this process but also recognize that their writing process is their own and might deviate slightly from the recursive cycle of this one. Coaching students to figure out how they like to brainstorm or when in the process they like to begin revision is work that transcends the genre and is ultimately helpful to writers in everything from crafting literary essays to drafting important emails. We want writers to own their process … and continue to refine it.

Inside of this work you'll want to emphasize how writers turn to mentor texts across the writing process, so that your writers, no matter what genre they are working on, and where they are in the writing process, know they can seek mentor texts to help them raise the level of their writing. Here, you'll see that we include mentor text lessons to help students get to know the genre, to study how writers structure memoirs, what kind of literary craft published writers use to enhance their memoirs, and what modalities they publish in.

Turning to Mentor Texts Across the Writing Process

Researching & Collecting	Planning & Drafting	Revising & Raising the Level	Getting Ready to Publish
• Getting to know the genre • Gathering ideas for content • Envisioning ways to publish	• Imagining possible structures • Deconstructing 'parts' inside this genre • Studying beginnings and endings	• Finding ideas for craft techniques • Mirror writing at the sentence level • Studying authorial voice and how it is achieved	• Revisiting conventions • Envisioning modalities • Considering specific audiences

Access a collection of mentor memoirs at hs-guidetoteaching.org.

We've included a writing process checklist, as these are very high-leverage habits that will support your students long after they have left your classroom.

One note about collecting and generating: early on, when your students are finding ideas for stories, make sure they don't only jot and talk, but also write the beginnings of their stories. We traditionally have had students jot in notebooks, and we call these *notebook entries* or *writing*. The notebook is simply a metaphor for the place you are working on your writing, and for some students, that may be an iPad or laptop. *Freewriting* describes the process of starting a story, or a bit of writing, without worrying that you'll finish it. The main thing is, before they choose the story they want to draft, students should collect a few short *entries* or *freewrites*, so they have material to work from.

A note, as well, about publishing: we suggest that students choose among several modalities, but, of course, you could choose a single modality that your students will publish in. For instance, all your students could publish their memoirs in anthologies or as picture books. We love choice because it leads to higher engagement, but sometimes choice is hard to manage. Talk to your students, and your colleagues, and consider what works best for your writers and their teacher.

Revision and Writing Process Checklist:
Some High-Leverage Writing Habits

Pre-Writing:
as evidenced in my notebook or folder

- ☐ I researched my own life thinking about issues, motifs, pre-occupations, and moments.
- ☐ I generated multiple possible ideas, creating maps, writing quick introductions to pieces, and ________.

Use of Mentor Texts:
as evidenced by annotated texts

- ☐ I studied mentor texts to get to know the genre, finding one or two as possible mentors.
- ☐ I studied mentor texts as a writer, investigating:
  - ☐ memoir structures.
  - ☐ craft techniques.
  - ☐ artful conventions.
  - ☐ publishing modalities.

Goal-Setting, Planning, and Drafting:
as evidenced by lean plans, marked up texts, early drafts

- ☐ I used exemplars, checklists, mentor texts, and/or prior pieces to set goals for my writing.
- ☐ I did some thoughtful planning about overall structure and how my piece would go before drafting.

Evidence of Revision:
as evidenced by multiple draft versions

- ☐ I was careful to keep track of my revision, perhaps by:
  - ☐ recording my verbal rehearsal.
  - ☐ keeping multiple tabs or versions of my piece.
  - ☐ color coding my revisions.
  - ☐ tracking my revision as I uploaded it to an EdTech partner.
- ☐ My final piece shows evidence of revision such as:
  - ☐ developing meaning.
  - ☐ trying craft techniques.
  - ☐ artful conventions.

Supporting and Celebrating Multilingual Students and Newcomers

We teach and coach in bilingual classrooms, in classrooms full of newcomers, in international classrooms where every student is multilingual, in classrooms where the teacher is monolingual and the students have a dozen languages among them, in classrooms where only a few students are learning English or the classroom language, and everything in between. What we know for sure is that we want to create communities of care and belonging, and we want to institute structures that will both reveal and extend students' linguistic competencies.

In their gorgeous book, *En Comunidad: Lessons for Centering the Voices and Experiences of Bilingual Latinx Students*, Carla España and Luz Yadira Herrera describe a primary pedagogical goal when teaching multilingual students: "to embrace their full linguistic repertoire" (2020, xvii). For us, part of that work lies in making strategic decisions about curriculum and texts—choosing texts that mirror the identities and experiences of our students, making sure there is rich representation in the mentor texts and authors students encounter. But there is more. We also try to focus on our interactions and our structures. In our interactions, we follow Ofelia García's advice to embrace translanguaging as a) a natural part of linguistic development and b) a way for students to express themselves with more nuance (García and Kleyn 2016; García et al. 2017).

We add in using AI, a newer development, as a tool for students to translate. With this tool, we can read a memoir written by a student who has come from Ukraine yesterday, and we can respond as well, crossing language differences to know our students and communicate with them and their families more deeply. Our multilingual students, even as they learn a new language, can express their thinking in the language they are most powerful in, so their learning continues at multiple levels and they show their full competencies (Ehrenworth and Seyfried 2025).

Becoming Adept and Ethical with AI

You'll see that we include a lesson in every part of the writing process on wise ways to turn to AI. OpenAI, and most EdTech AI, can give remarkably expert, insightful feedback to students, in a kind and affirming tone that young writers need. And teens need to learn why *not* to turn the work of drafting over to AI—both for ethical reasons and also so that AI trains them to become more powerful writers, rather than replacing them. In each lesson, we emphasize how to train an AI partner—how to give it a lot of information, so that its feedback and suggestions are personalized to that writer. We also continually teach students how to reference AI support, in a footnote, an endnote, or an acknowledgment. We believe we have an ethical responsibility to teach students about the ways writers use AI, in learning environments that allow students to play in the AI sandbox.

For the lessons in this book, you can set up EdTech AI chat partners, such as MagicSchool or Flint, or you can teach students how adults use OpenAI, depending on your school policies. If you want to think more deeply about the future role of AI and writing, we encourage you to read *AI-Enhanced Literacy: Practical Steps for Deepening Reading and Writing Instruction* (Ehrenworth and Seyfried 2025) and *Co-Intelligence: Living and Working with AI* (Mollick 2024). We do recommend that students have EdTech AI partners, as otherwise, they will seek OpenAI, and you won't be able to advise them or shape those interactions.

One more note about AI, in regard to translation. Because the goal of memoir is for students to be seen and heard, it may be that some multilingual students, especially newcomers, will write a memoir in the language in which they have the most competence, and use AI to translate it for their readers. We believe in using technology to grasp students' competencies and fully see all our students.

Final Thoughts

Time with our students is precious, and there is never enough of it, so we think it's worth noting how powerful it is that you've dedicated time to memoir, to story. Most state and global standards ask us to teach narrative techniques, knowing that narrative writers become better narrative readers, and narrative craft infuses every genre. Yet narrative writing is much more than learning technique. Telling our stories creates community and builds empathy and prompts deep reflection.

It is hard to be young, and it is harder for some children and some families than for others in ways that we might not easily notice. Storytelling helps our young people see and be seen. Anne Lamott, in *Bird by Bird* (2019), reminds us that "we are a species that needs and wants to understand who we are." National Ambassador for Young People's Literature, Jason Reynolds (2024) asserts, "I really believe that every person walking this earth has a story." He goes on to talk about storytelling as "a bit of a meander." So much of school forbids meandering.

You are about to wander a bit off the path, into your students' stories, and they are going to wander into yours, and it is in those unexpected places that we find each other.

Chapter One: Finding Our Stories

You would think that finding ideas to write about would be an especially easy task when you are writing about your own life. Many teens, though, are unsure that their life is worth writing about. Our first job, then, is to convince them that yes, their life is full of quirky and interesting moments, that in their everyday interactions they bump into social issues, they challenge preconceptions, they outgrow themselves. Adolescence is a time of paradoxes, traumas, and epiphanies. Teens experience combustible levels of stress. and often have little control over their lives. Memoir writing can help teens manage these stressors. Lisa Damour (2019) speaks of how stress is crucial to change, and change is essential to growth. She speaks of helping teens develop systems to reflect on and respond to the stress in their lives. Memoir is one such system, and it does more than help teens manage trouble; it also illuminates the small beauties in their lives as well.

In this chapter, you'll find lessons teaching a variety of strategies for finding ideas to write about. You may be surprised that the first strategy sets up students with an AI partner. You'll find, though, that when an AI partner learns a little information about a student (part of the lesson teaches students how to personalize the feedback they get from an AI partner), it can respond with surprising warmth and humanity, dousing students with affirmation that their lives are the seeds of written stories. The confidence that comes from that interaction often positions students to tackle this genre with more confidence.

You'll also find lessons that teach students to map and sketch and to think about places, social issues, and symbols. You might combine some of these lessons as a series of micro lessons, or you might choose a few that you think will best match your students. One lesson that we recommend you teach to all students is Lesson 2, which is an inquiry into the different ways memoir can look, including written memoirs, spoken-word performances, video narratives, and picture books. It can be very powerful, at the start of a genre, to preview what published pieces can look like—when writers have a vision of what they want to achieve, they can work toward that vision with more agency. You'll also find that teens are inspired by other young people who have told their stories in courageous ways.

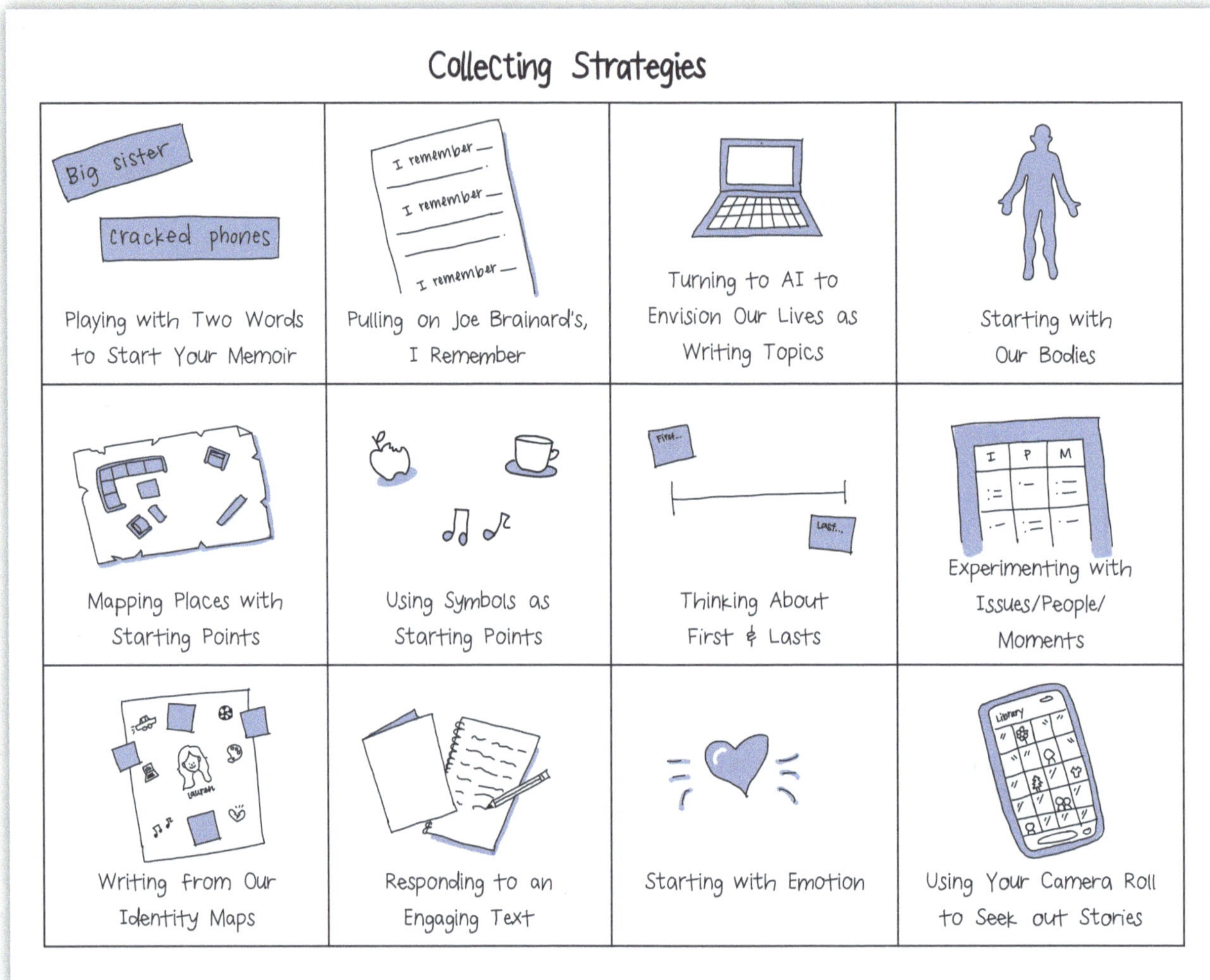

It can be helpful for students to collect multiple moments as possible writing ideas, both because they may decide to put some of these moments together, and because they often begin to see patterns in their experiences. You can embed these same patterns in your demonstration writing, so that students see you take risks, reflect, and come to new realizations. Mary, for instance, tends to write about her struggles to fit in with a wealthier, more popular clique at school; about love; and about sports. Lauren tends to write about her role as responsible older sister juxtaposed with her desire to rebel. Coley tends to write about navigating tricky friendships and romantic relationships. Our students, then, can begin to give us advice about patterns they notice in our storytelling, which allows our class to act as writing partners to us.

Your students will share their ideas through oral storytelling, sketching, and freewriting. As they do this work, you want to model what affirmative partnership looks like. Circulate, leaning over students' shoulders, saying phrases that stir them up to want to write.

One note: all of these collecting strategies lead students to jot ideas and then tell their stories to their partners. Be sure to immediately follow up with some time for students to freewrite one or two notebook entries as well (digitally or in an old-fashioned notebook). These entries will be the start of possible stories. Once writers have gathered at least two or three entries, then they can think about which story they most want to tell, and/or if they want to combine more than one for a memoir. We tend to call these short drafts *entries* or *freewrites*.

Things we can say to our writing partners as they find their stories...

- You have to write that!
- I love that story!
- It makes me feel/think...
- It reminds me of...
- What an important topic!
- Other kids will really appreciate...
- It feels like maybe your story is about...

Lesson 1

Turning to AI to Spark Stories

STRATEGY

Experienced AI users know that AI can be surprisingly personal and helpful in helping writers find topics. To explore memoir topics, writers tell their AI partner something about themselves, usually focusing on a particular period in their life, and they ask their AI partner for help shaping that information into possible writing topics.

USE THIS STRATEGY...early in the writing process, when writers are just getting started with their memoirs and would love some help finding moments in their lives to write about. Also use it when your writers would benefit from personal affirmation that their lives are worth writing about.

TEACH THE STRATEGY

- Suggest to students that AI can be a surprisingly intimate and generous writing partner, able to validate writer's ideas and find writing ideas in their life experiences.
- Set up an EdTech AI partner, such as Flint, MagicSchool, or SchoolAI, to support students in finding ideas for their memoirs, or set up students with ChatGPT or Claude.
    - Direct the EdTech AI partner to ask writers to tell it a bit about themselves and to suggest possible personalized topics, titles, and themes.
    - Direct students using OpenAI to explain to their AI partner the help they are seeking.

To Find Ideas for Your Memoir, Prompt AI By....

- sharing important parts of your identity.
- offering up hobbies, sports, clubs, ways you spend your time.
- describing important people and relationships.
- expressing issues and fears that come up for you.
- avoiding the sharing of personal identifiers (if using OpenAI).

- Model for students how you first tell your AI partner that you are looking for memoir ideas, and then share personal information with an AI partner so that it can personalize its response with this knowledge. Choose an age (near that of the students you teach), and demonstrate sharing some personal information. Angle this information to hint at issues or feelings that your students might share.
- Study your AI partner's suggestions, voicing over how some of the topics resonate with you as possible starting points. You might combine topic suggestions, or zoom in on part of one, to show how these are meant to get you started. You can also invite students to suggest which ones they'd like to read, as an audience.
- Guide students to use their AI partner to generate memoir ideas, and then to choose one or two to try drafting as a notebook entry or freewrite.

PROMPTS TO COACH STUDENTS AND PARTNERSHIPS

Tell your AI partner about different parts of your life—maybe how you spend your time outside of school, what your favorite films or books or music is and why, or what preoccupies you or worries you. Get personal with this private partner!

Sometimes it's easier to share information and issues from when you were younger—a lot of memoirists do that.

You might look over the suggestions your AI partner makes with your writing partner, to see which topics seem intriguing, to you as a writer and your partner as a reader.

CLASSROOM ARTIFACTS

I am getting started with writing a memoir and am looking for topic ideas from my life. As an eighth and ninth grader, I spent a lot of time in a nearby stables, helping with the horses. I really wanted to ride, and even own a horse, but we couldn't afford lessons - and definitely not a horse. So I would trade taking care of the horses and cleaning the stables for lessons. I also spent a lot of time in the library, mostly reading fantasy series like Narnia and Lord of the Rings - I think I liked the escape, maybe because I never felt like I fit in perfectly at school. I was a little afraid of the popular kids, who always seemed like they had better clothes (Izod shirts), bigger houses, and fancier vacations. Can you help me with some memoir ideas with this information?

Mary shares intimate (but not traumatic) information with her AI partner in her demo.

Mary's AI partner, for instance, made these suggestions:

Here are some memoir topic ideas based on your experiences:

1. **"Trading Muck for Magic"** – A story about your determination to ride despite financial barriers, how working in the stables shaped your resilience, and the contrast between your dreams and reality.
2. **"The Smell of Horses and the Sound of Pages"** – A reflection on how both the stables and the library offered you different kinds of escape and belonging, showing the parallel between fantasy worlds and the barn world.
3. **"Izods and Saddles"** – A piece exploring your feelings about social class and fitting in, juxtaposing the world of "popular kids" with your own identity and the fulfillment you found in horses and books.
4. **"Invisible in the Saddle"** – How riding horses gave you a sense of power and belonging that you didn't always feel at school, and the ways in which both animals and stories gave you confidence.
5. **"Cleaning Stalls, Dreaming Castles"** – A memoir piece connecting the gritty, hands-on work of caring for horses with the epic adventures you read about, highlighting themes of perseverance and longing for something bigger.
6. **"The Girl in the Library Corner"** – A deep dive into why you loved fantasy, what those stories gave you emotionally, and how they shaped your understanding of the world and yourself.

Mary's AI partner offered these suggestions.

Lesson 2

Memoir Mentor Text Immersion

STRATEGY

Because memoir writers don't follow one set pattern, structure, or even modality, it's helpful (and inspiring) to study memoirs that look and feel different, thinking: How might I want my own memoir to go?

Visit hs-guidetoteaching.org to access a collection of mentors.

USE THIS STRATEGY...to deepen and broaden the vision of what memoir is, and to help students see the variety of ways memoir might look and sound, so they find their own path, as well as envision the modality they might publish in later.

> **Inquiry Question**
>
> What moves does this writer make that I like or admire?
> What does this writer do that I might want to try?

LAUNCH THE INQUIRY

- Suggest to students that it's always worth it, when launching into a genre, to study examples of that genre to learn more about it.
- Set students up with a collection of mentor memoirs. We've included a list of both print and digital (spoken word/animated/graphic) memoirs we especially like.
- Engage students in watching/reading one memoir together and naming what's powerful about it.

Mary modeled with "The Saint of Dry Creek," an animated memoir by Patrick Haggerty that is available on YouTube. With student input, Mary noted the way the story built in surprising ways, so that what looked like was going to be a story about Pat's drama performance ends up being a story about his relationship with his dad and his dad's surprising acceptance and wisdom about Pat's sexuality.

A Collection of Mentor Memoirs

Graphic Novel Memoirs

- *El Deafo* by Cece Bell
- *Fun Home by* Alison Bechdel
- *I Was Their American Dream* by Malaka Gharib
- *Rosalie Lightning* by Tom Hart
- *Persepolis* by Marjane Satrapi
- *They Called Us Enemy* by George Takei

Spoken Word Memoirs

- "Hair" by Elizabeth Acevedo
- "Gummi Bears Forever" by Matt Dicks
- "The Bad Haircut" by Alfonso Lacayo
- "This Body" by Renee Watson

Other Multimedia

- "El Deafo — A Note from the Author," Cece Bell
- "Dear Basketball" by Kobe Bryant
- "The Saint of Dry Creek" by Patrick Haggerty

Excerpts/Chapters

- Sandra Cisneros, stories from *House on Mango Street*
- Sandra Cisneros, stories from *Woman Hollering Creek*
- Naomi Shihab Nye"s, "Gate A4"
- David Sidaris, "Big Boy," from *Me Talk Pretty One Day*
- Misa Sugiura, "Where I'm From" from *Come on In*
- Jacqueline Woodson, poems from *Brown Girl Dreaming*

Books

- *I'm Glad my Mom Died* by Jennette McCurdy
- *Born a Crime: YA Version* by Trevor Noah
- *Educated* by Tara Westover
- *Solito* by Javier Zamora
- *Crying in H Mart* by Michelle Zauner

Picture Books

- *Birdsong*, written & illustrated by Julie Flett
- *Areli Is a Dreamer*, written by Areli Morales & illustrated by Luisa Uribe
- *My Papi has a Motorcycle*, written by Isabel Quintero & illustrated by Zeke Peña
- *A Different Pond*, written by Bao Phi & illustrated by Thi Bui
- *Watercress*, written Andrew Wang & illustrated by Jason Chin

- Send students off, in partnerships or small groups, to immerse themselves in all different memoirs, asking students to consider the structure and the style.
  - ♦ You might organize picture books, printed pages, books, and laptops all around the classroom, so students can move around in stations.
- There may or may not be time remaining for students to write. If there is time, encourage them to freewrite in response to one of these, jotting what piece they most responded to, and why.

PROMPTS TO COACH STUDENTS AND PARTNERSHIPS

Don't linger forever in one mentor—read or watch a few, so you'll have more ideas about what a memoir might look like.

Some authors give you new ideas for form—what mode you might like to publish in—and others give you ideas for content as well—what you might write about.

If you already know what kind of writing you tend to do, more funny, more serious, lighter or darker, then you can also look for mentors in that tone.

CLASSROOM ARTIFACTS

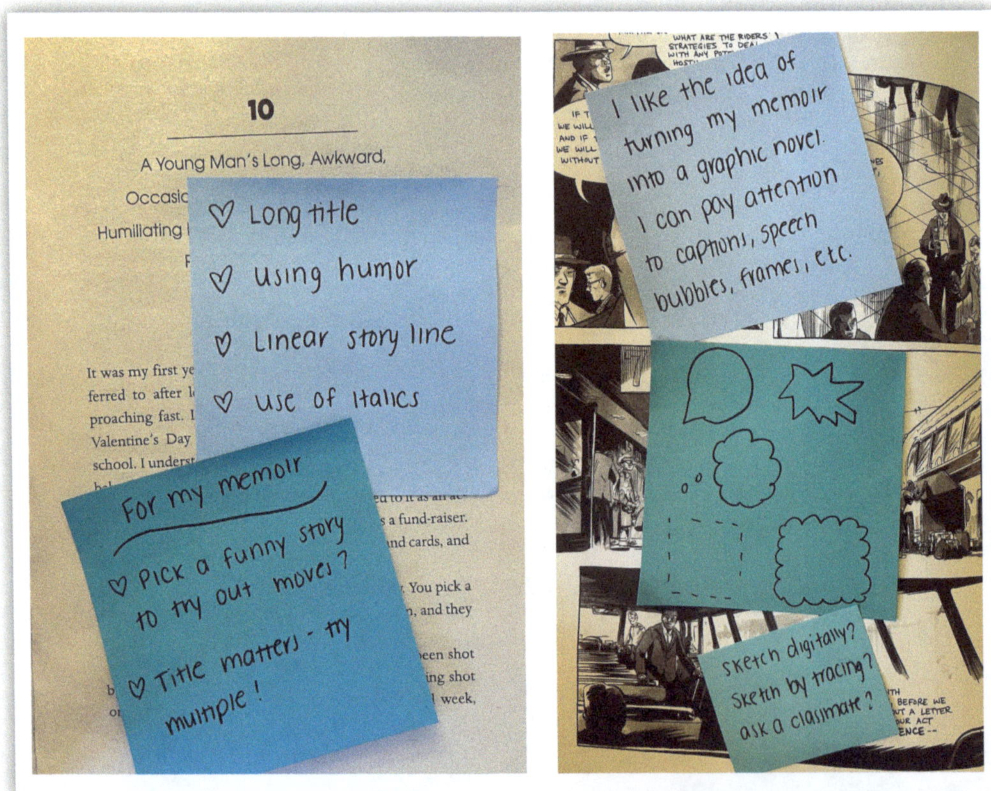

Writers study mentor texts, noting what resonates with them.

Lesson 3

Firsts and Lasts

STRATEGY

Writers often turn to firsts and last: the first time they felt or realized or experienced something, or the last time they did. Often, it's interesting to think about *why* a moment matters—what realizations the writer felt upon a first experience, or what the writer misses about a last experience. First times might also include the first time they experienced/became aware of social issues and norms.

USE THIS STRATEGY...to support students in finding moments in their lives to write about. It's an especially helpful strategy in leading students to think about *why* a moment matters—what it is really about.

TEACH THE STRATEGY

- Suggest that thinking about firsts and lasts can help memoirists find ideas for their stories.
- Share an example of thinking about firsts or lasts to show what this strategy can lead to. For example, Ralph Fletcher, in *Marshfield Dreams* (2012), tells the story of the last time his father kissed him goodnight, because he was no longer a small child, and how he didn't know it would be the last.
- Model jotting some sticky notes as you think back over possible firsts and lasts. Choose moments that will resonate with your students and those that bring up shared experiences, emotions, or issues.

First slow dance with Chris, at 6th grade dance, to Led Zepplins Stairway to Heaven.

First time I realized gender mattered- summer of 9th grade, biking home with Kristy from pool, man waiting for us on the road.

Last time I remember not caring what people think- monkey bars at recess, grade 3.

- Unpack your moments, asking yourself why these matter and what these moments might really be about.

> Mary, for instance, talked about the awkwardness of crushes, how they paralyze you so you can barely function; how she felt when she realized that a lot of males are a lot stronger than females, especially teenagers; and what it felt like to try to be the fastest and strongest in recess, in elementary school, even against boys.

- Invite students to think about firsts and lasts in their own lives, jotting their ideas first then telling their stories to a partner. Then invite them to freewrite one or two moments as a notebook entry.

PROMPTS TO COACH STUDENTS AND PARTNERSHIPS

Sometimes you can think about something that you do now that's important to you, like soccer or piano, and you can think back—what's your first memory of doing that?

It can be interesting to think about things you used to love to do when you were young, like collecting Pokémon or playing with a pet, and then think why that thing mattered to you.

When you think about first times, these can be hard realizations or intimate moments that you might want to talk about with just your partner.

CLASSROOM ARTIFACTS

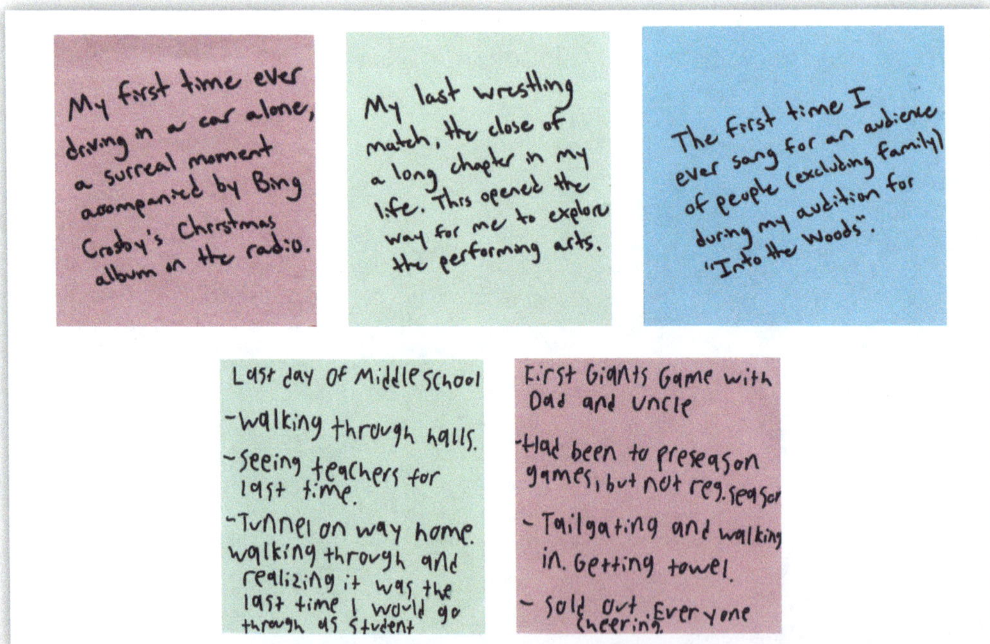

Students collect memories of "firsts and lasts" to extract ideas for their memoirs.

Symbols as Starting Points

Lesson 4

STRATEGY

Memoirists often find it useful to think about things that are symbolic in their lives, like particular food, music, sayings, events, or objects. Often these things hold parts of their identities, and they make good starting points for finding stories that are about not only the writer but also their lives, cultures, and families.

USE THIS STRATEGY...to lead students toward moments that are full of possible cultural reflection. Often students find foods to be full of significance for their family and heritage. Others find certain sayings, or events, significant. This strategy often leads students toward moments that are redolent and suggestive.

Visit hs-guidetoteaching.org to download the chart and access a collection of mentor texts to showcase this strategy.

TEACH THE STRATEGY

- Introduce the notion of symbols in our lives, sharing a chart of things that can often be symbolic, such as foods, events, music, sayings, and objects.

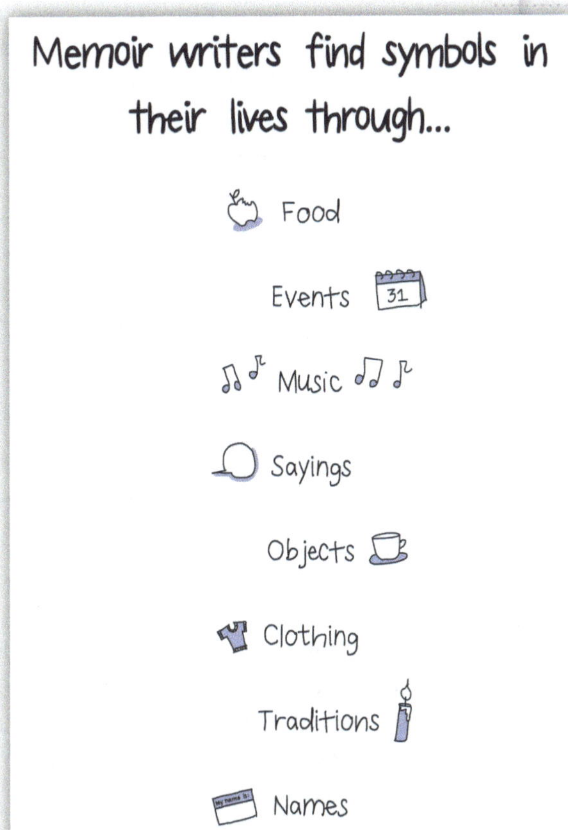

- Share a snippet of an example. We suggest the poem "Trading Places" from *Brown Girl Dreaming*, Jacqueline Woodson's memoir (2014). We also love George Ella Lyon's poem, "Where I'm From" (1993), asking students to consider the symbols that are present in these texts and what they might represent.
    - In the excerpt, "Trading Places," Jacqueline describes how her friend Maria's mother makes *arroz con habichuelas y tostones*, while hers makes chicken and corn bread, and how they would trade dinners—an act of friendship, of cultural exchange, of love.

Lesson 4 (Continued)

- ♦ In her poem, George Ella Lyon recalls clothespins and Clorox and the dirt under her back porch and turns these recollections of images into an evocative image of her youth that shaped her identity.

- You might model for a moment, demonstrating something that feels particularly symbolic to you, from your childhood, your family history, or your culture.

Collecting Story Ideas: Symbols

Food

- Cheeseburgers and steak fries
- Crumb cakes*
- Ice cream
- Pearled onions
- Sweet and sour chicken

Free Writing: Crumb Cakes

My teeth were chattering and I couldn't feel my fingers in my gloves. It must have been the coldest day of the year. I had to take the numbness and the burn on my skin if I wanted to taste the buttery goodness of a Diorses crumb cake. It was 6:30am and just like every Wednesday morning, my Pop-Pop and I waited in the never-ending line outside the bakery. Of course, these weren't just crumb cakes. These were the best crumb cakes 80% crumb, 20% cake. Not dusted with powdered sugar, but glazed in a sweet frosting.

I looked at the long line of people in front of us and asked my Pop-Pop, "What if there aren't any left?"

"There will be." he reassured me. "There always are."

Each minute we inched closer and closer to the door. The sun rose as we finally made it inside. I ran in and pressed my nose against the warm glass.

Notes: Pop-pop- ritual- always took me to school- this was Kindergarten.-- eventually got too old. Wish I went for him- I never did.

Coley, for instance, brainstormed different foods that hold meaning in her life. Then she looked for patterns, noticing that the food she has specific memories around all represent her relationship with her Pop-Pop. She wrote to think more deeply about this symbol.

- Invite students to open their notebooks/computers and do some freewriting about possible symbols, and then to talk through these moments with a partner.

PROMPTS TO COACH STUDENTS AND PARTNERSHIPS

When gathering symbols, it almost always works to think about food—it could be food from family car trips, or special meals that bring the family together or that are particularly important in your family.

Sometimes you can find symbolism in an object—a ribbon or award or an old toy. Music can bring up lots of memories, like moments when you especially remember listening to that song.

Now that you have a few symbols, think about what they represent. What patterns do you notice? What deeper meaning do these hold? What stories live within the symbol?

CLASSROOM ARTIFACTS

Free write #1

When I was ten, my brothers, cousins, and dad went to Munich to watch a favorite player, Bastian Schweinsteiger, from our favorite club, Bayern Munich, play. We all stayed in a hotel together. It was such a thing, to have all of us in one place. The best part was the meal we had. After the game, we returned to where my dad is originally from-a small town near Stuttgart. We ate currywurst from a local shop. I wish we could be together more, like that, in these perfect moments of connection.

Free write #2

Wherever we are, we are a family of eating. We LOVE Thanksgiving. It's not just the food, although we take that seriously. It's also that our family isn't together that much, so this is our time. When my dad and I moved to Barcelona, it separated all of us. Since then, I only see my brothers in the summers, or sometimes well meet for a vacation. So, a time like Thanksgiving is important. Ive learned, from these experiences, to value times like these, and also to work to create them. Ive learned how important it is to forge connections across barriers.

Trying a freewrite two ways can reveal multiple meanings for the same symbol.

Free Write

I look forward to eating my favorite foods that my mom only cooks on Christmas since it takes hours to make and prep. From the second I wake up I can smell the cinnamony Rabanadas (a Portuguese french toast dessert) cooking downstairs. I look forward to skyping my insanely loud relatives in Portugal since everyone there is together and I get to see my whole family in one room. Part of me always gets jealous of those long-distance skype calls since Ive never been able to experience a "traditional" Christmas. Although there is a small part of me that wishes I was born in Portugal so I could experience my "traditional" Christmas, celebrating holidays with just my mom, dad, sister and it has brought us closer than most families which I value a lot more than the presents under the tree.

This writer freewrites about holiday traditions.

Lesson 5

Starting with Our Bodies

STRATEGY

Our bodies—including all the ways we feel about them, the ways we feel judged or celebrated, parts that we love and don't love—can be intimate topics for memoir. Sometimes it helps to see what other memoirists have written, to see how they speak in narrative or reflective ways about parts of their bodies.

Visit hs-guidetoteaching.org for a current collection of fabulous memoir mentors/excerpts, including these videos.

USE THIS STRATEGY...to introduce more gorgeous voices to your students, including Elizabeth Acevedo and Renée Watson, and to tap into adolescents' strong feelings about their bodies, as a source for memoir.

TEACH THE STRATEGY

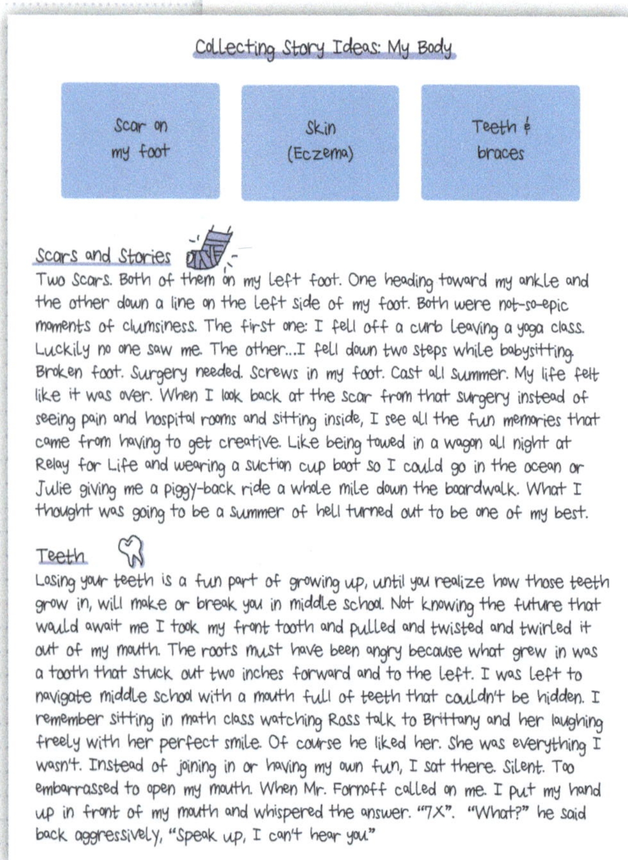
Collecting Story Ideas: My Body

Scar on my foot	Skin (Eczema)	Teeth & braces

Scars and Stories

Two Scars. Both of them on my left foot. One heading toward my ankle and the other down a line on the left side of my foot. Both were not-so-epic moments of clumsiness. The first one: I fell off a curb leaving a yoga class. Luckily no one saw me. The other...I fell down two steps while babysitting. Broken foot. Surgery needed. Screws in my foot. Cast all summer. My life felt like it was over. When I look back at the scar from that surgery instead of seeing pain and hospital rooms and sitting inside, I see all the fun memories that came from having to get creative. Like being towed in a wagon all night at Relay for Life and wearing a suction cup boot so I could go in the ocean or Julie giving me a piggy-back ride a whole mile down the boardwalk. What I thought was going to be a summer of hell turned out to be one of my best.

Teeth

Losing your teeth is a fun part of growing up, until you realize how those teeth grow in, will make or break you in middle school. Not knowing the future that would await me I took my front tooth and pulled and twisted and twirled it out of my mouth. The roots must have been angry because what grew in was a tooth that stuck out two inches forward and to the left. I was left to navigate middle school with a mouth full of teeth that couldn't be hidden. I remember sitting in math class watching Ross talk to Brittany and her laughing freely with her perfect smile. Of course he liked her. She was everything I wasn't. Instead of joining in or having my own fun, I sat there. Silent. Too embarrassed to open my mouth. When Mr. Fornoff called on me. I put my hand up in front of my mouth and whispered the answer. "7X". "What?" he said back aggressively, "Speak up, I can't hear you"

- Suggest to students that memoir writers often find ideas for things they love and don't love by thinking about their (and other's) relationship with their bodies.
- Introduce Renée Watson's "This Body," and invite students to talk about lines they liked, what emotions she expresses, what she says. (Visit hs-guidetoteaching.org or YouTube.)
- Introduce and show Elizabeth Acevedo's "Hair," and similarly invite students to talk about the piece. You might find you want to play parts more than once. (Visit hs-guidetoteaching.org or YouTube.)
- Demonstrate how you might think about some part of your body that you loved/didn't love or made you feel celebrated or judged, and do some quick freewriting as a model.
- Invite students to try this strategy as a starting point for some memoir ideas. Encourage them to do some freewriting and then to share with a partner.

When Coley explored these memoir performances with her students, she jotted a few sticky notes as starting points, thinking about the complexities of her own relationship with her body, specifically as a teenager. Then, she did some freewriting about these topics in her notebook.

PROMPTS TO COACH STUDENTS AND PARTNERSHIPS

It's interesting how Acevedo turns her hair into something symbolic, a symbol of defiance. You can do that too, thinking about how some part of you symbolizes something bigger about your childhood.

Both Acevedo and Watson explore how they felt about their bodies, and how others did, and they get at some tension there. Those tensions can be interesting starting points.

You can think about your body on the outside, but also on the inside. Consider what you have to say about your mind … or your heart.

CLASSROOM ARTIFACTS

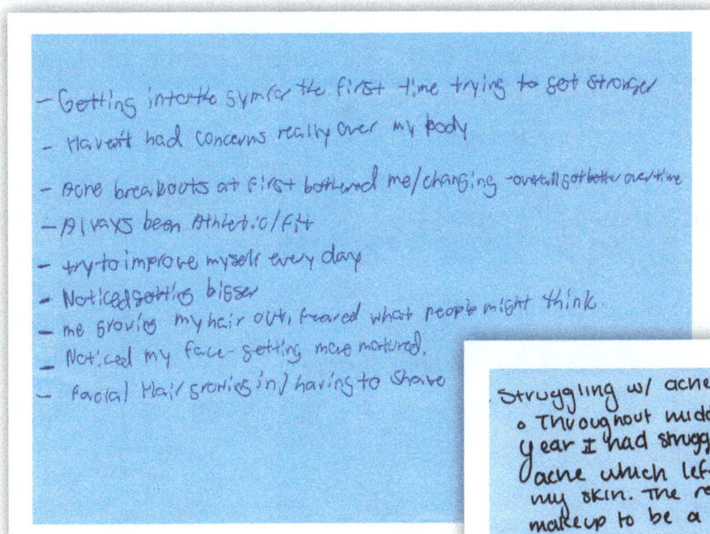

- Getting into the gym for the first time trying to get stronger
- Haven't had concerns really over my body
- Acne breakouts at first bothered me/changing -overall got better over time
- Always been Athletic/Fit
- try to improve myself every day
- Noticed getting bigger
- me growing my hair out, feared what people might think.
- Noticed my face getting more matured.
- Facial Hair growing in, having to shave

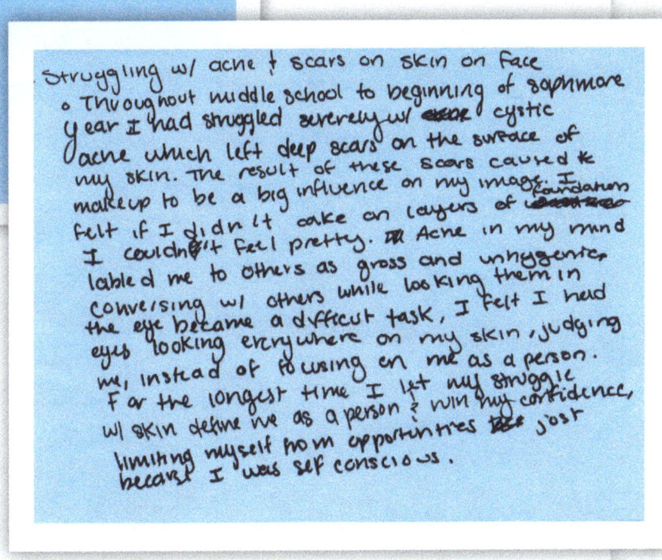

Struggling w/ acne & scars on skin on face
∘ Throughout middle school to beginning of sophmore year I had struggled severely w/ cystic acne which left deep scars on the surface of my skin. The result of these scars caused makeup to be a big influence on my image. I felt if I didn't cake on layers of foundation I couldn't feel pretty. Acne in my mind labled me to others as gross and unhygenic conversing w/ others while looking them in the eye became a difficut task, I felt I had eyes looking everywhere on my skin, judging me, instead of focusing on me as a person. For the longest time I let my struggle w/ skin define me as a person & win my confidence, just limiting myself from opportunities because I was self conscious.

These teens reflect on their bodies as a way to collect ideas for memoirs.

Lesson 6

Exploring Issues, People, and Moments

STRATEGY

All writers know that lists help writers hold onto multiple ideas. When collecting ideas for memoir, it can be helpful to list issues and people, and then think of *moments of strong emotions* attached to these. It's also helpful to ask of each moment: What else is this story about? Often there may be multiple issues hiding in a single moment.

USE THIS STRATEGY...to demonstrate for students how one story idea often leads to another. This strategy also leads students to unpack multiple underlying motifs in their moments—any moment that is about more than one thing is going to be an intriguing, complicated memoir topic.

TEACH THE STRATEGY

- Suggest to students that there are often issues hiding in our lives that will lead to powerful writing. One way to find these issues is to think of moments of strong emotion and what issues might underlie these moments.
- Demonstrate how you might get started with this strategy, jotting and voicing over as you write, to bring students into your process. Jot a rough chart of Issues/People/Moments, and begin with an issue or a person that occupied your emotions when you were young. Think aloud about some moments of particularly strong emotions.

Collecting Story Ideas:
Issues, People, Moments

Issue	People	Moments
• Friendship • Betrayal • Jealousy	• Lisa • Chris	• Mud brownies
• Fitting in • Status	• Lisa • The popular kids	• Alligator shirt moment
• Fitting in • Having an accent when we moved	• Hilary	• "We can't understand you"

Mary, for instance, thought about Lisa, who was her best friend growing up. She began by jotting "friendship" as an issue, next to "Lisa," and then voiced over thinking about times when she felt great with Lisa, and times she didn't. Then she told the story of when they were very young and Lisa tricked her into eating mud brownies as a way of impressing a new boy, Chris. Asking, "what else is this story about" led to "betrayal" and "jealousy." Then, Mary showed how she didn't have another mud brownie story, but she did have more stories about betrayal, and she told the story of when Lisa wouldn't let her sit with the popular kids in the cafeteria, because Mary didn't have a Lacoste shirt with an alligator on it. From there, that story led to issues of fitting in and status.

In your demonstration, focus on moments when you were young and issues that many kids will relate to.

- Invite students to do some listing. Encourage them to collect two or three moments, and then tell their partner one or two of their stories. If there is time, they can freewrite the start of one or two stories.

PROMPTS TO COACH STUDENTS AND PARTNERSHIPS

Often it helps to start with something you do all the time, or someone you spent a lot of time with, like teammates or siblings. Then you ask yourself: When have I felt really great, and when have I felt not-so-great with this person, or doing this thing?

Push your partner to find specific moments. Make them start with, "I remember the moment when …"

Any moment that is about more than one issue is going to be a good moment to write about.

CLASSROOM ARTIFACTS

People	Emotions/Issues	Moments
Kendall	Embarrassment Lying Good times- middle school	Our lying moments- even recently with her
Mom	Disappointment in my grades– under appreciated.	Calling mom to talk about grades when she's taking care of grandma– didn't go well.
Yankee (Dog)	My forgetfulness with walks	Always waiting by door but forget to go straight home- then think of him and feel bad.
Monroy	Being mean and feeling bad	Best friend, but moments when I take things too far. Moments of support system, like with grades.

This writer tries out the strategy.

Lesson 7

Mapping Places to Unearth Stories

STRATEGY

When writers are seeking ideas for memoir writing, they often return to places, especially those that inspire strong emotions. One way that writers develop their thinking about place is mapping, including maps that link places with identities, issues, and emotions.

USE THIS STRATEGY... as a highly accessible starting place for finding stories. Some writers might map a single room or building, while others map neighborhoods or summer camps.

Visit hs-guidetoteaching.org to download sample maps.

TEACH THE STRATEGY

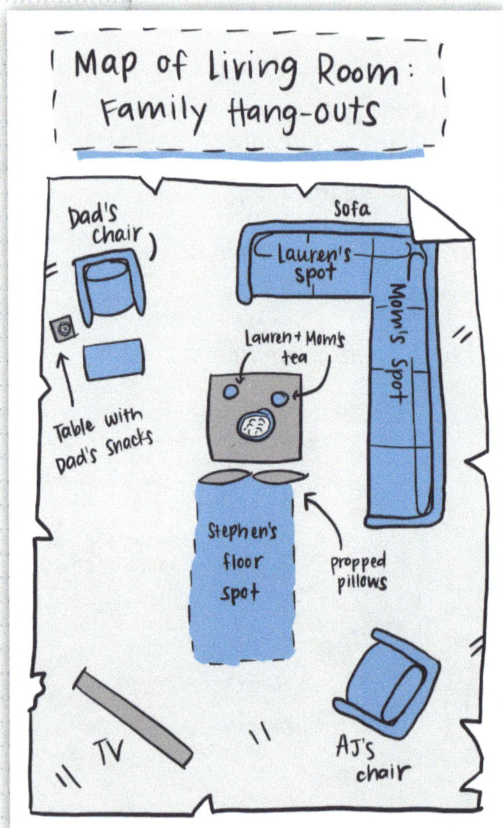

- Suggest to writers that often our stories are hiding in familiar places, where we've had many experiences.
- Invite students to think about place, especially in terms of place as an emotional site, where feelings linger in our memories. Suggest that maps can explore identity, social issues, and strong emotions.
- You might show Malaka Gharib's social map of Cerritos High (excerpted from *I Was Their American Dream* (2019)) as an example. We also find the collection, *The Quarantine Atlas* (Bliss et al. 2022), which is full of maps people sketched of where they lived during COVID-19, very moving.
- Sketch what your own map might look like. It might be summer camp, or your neighborhood, or part of the school—anyplace where your stories from childhood are hiding.

Lauren made a map of her living room—a room full of family memories. As she mapped out each spot, she collected story ideas that featured her family members. She also thought about family holidays and how the map of the room changed depending on the event.

- Invite students to sketch their own maps, encouraging them to consider specific places, like school, summer camps, or neighborhoods, where a lot of stories and a lot of strong emotions might be found.
- Remind students that once they sketch a map, they can move to freewriting.

PROMPTS TO COACH STUDENTS AND PARTNERSHIPS

You might start with just one room, like a locker room or the cafeteria.

Sometimes playing fields can be places where a lot of stories can be found.

You might have a place that you only get to visit rarely, which makes it all the more special.

CLASSROOM ARTIFACTS

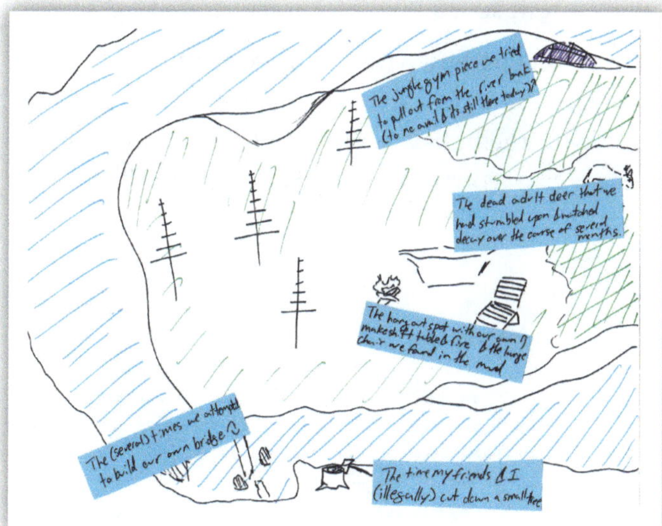

This writer maps a special place, then begins a story based off the map.

Sure, I ~~hade s~~ had seen dead things many times before in my life: a dead squirrel on the side of the road or a dead bird's wing snapped in half, but it was here that I had truly seen something rot – although, no, rot isn't a great word. Maybe decay; rot carries too negative of a connotation whereas there was something almost elegant & peaceful about the sight that we had stumbled upon. The others would probably disagree, but oh well. You see, it was quite a shock to come across. The others had to take a walk for a moment & the rest of us tip-toed around the corpse as we continued down the path. I think at the time I initially would have agreed with them, but as time passed & they moved on, I didn't. As we moved on to highschool & all found ourselves with better things to be doing, I found myself going back on my own. The space had become significantly quieter than it had once been, but that deer was still there. It always was, except; it never entirely was. I guess I hadn't exactly seen the decay happen in real time, but as each interval of time between my visits passed, the less of the deer remained. After a while it was eventually entirely gone with nothing left to show for it except some stray pieces of fuzzy fur. I miss it sometimes. ~~Occas~~ Occasionally, the more morbid parts of my mind wishes that I had kept a bone from it; perhaps even its skull, but instead it is a ghost town. I don't quite know why I wish that I held on to a bone or two, but I suppose the lack thereof & my continued persistence of searching simply goes to show that I'm the only

Lesson 8

Two- (or a Few-) Word Memoirs

STRATEGY

Matt de la Peña (2023) has described how often it can be intriguing for writers to describe their life in only two (or a few) words. They start by imagining a few different word pairings and then looking for stories across their lives, connected to those words.

USE THIS STRATEGY...when students are early on in collecting ideas for their memoirs, or when students are reluctant writers. This strategy starts with only two words, or just a few words, and can feel less overwhelming than other strategies.

TEACH THE STRATEGY

- Frame the idea of a two- or a few-word memoirs, by asking students to brainstorm an answer to this question: "When you look back at your life, what do you see if you were to describe it in two, or a few, words?" Try to stick with two words, or only a few, so it's very easy to start.
- Demonstrate this strategy by modeling how you brainstorm a few different word pairings. Explain how you're pulling out vivid images that often have multiple moments associated with them, like "cracked phones," and usually not pairing two general, descriptive words like "happy and joyful."

Collecting Story Ideas:
Two Word Memoir

Two Word Memoirs:

- big sister
- first wheels
- best friend
- belly laughter
- sharp elbows
- burnt marshmallows

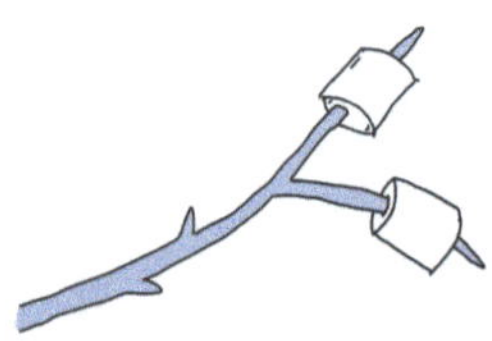

Burnt Marshmallows:

- camping with Laura
- making s'mores with my dad
- teaching my brothers to make s'mores
- getting marshmallow in my hair (always)
- making s'mores at camp with Megan
- helping my mom buy materials for s'mores
- finding gluten-free graham crackers after being diagnosed as celiac

Free Writing: Burnt Mashmallows

Summer tastes like s'mores. I don't remember the first s'more I ever made, but here's what I do remember: my best friend Laura at my side. Everytime our families went camping together, our quest was to make the best, crispy, perfect golden-brown marshmallow.

To do so, you first had to find a perfect spot between the logs in the fire. Next, you had to wait until the sugar in the marshmallow carmelized. This happened s-l-o-w-l-y. At first, it would turn a creamy yellow, then a light tan, and if you could wait long enough—if you could spin the stick without the 'mallow falling off—a perfect golden brown. Laura was a queen at this. Me? Mine always went up in flames.

I'd have to pull the flaming marshmallow torch out the fire and blow until it went out. Laura always joked that the black made for better flavor, but it just made me mad.

This is how things always seemed to go with me and Laura. She always had this knack of doing things perfectly on the first try. Things that would take me 3, or 10, or 20 times (or never!) to be able to do.

Lauren demonstrated this strategy. First, she generated possible titles for her two-word memoir. Then, she chose one title, "Burnt Marshmallows," and thought about times in her life that featured burnt marshmallows. Finally, she did some freewriting on this topic.

- Give students a few minutes to collect word pairings and then send them off to freewrite.

PROMPTS TO COACH STUDENTS AND PARTNERSHIPS

You might try making a timeline of your life, thinking of when these two words came up, and maybe talking out some of these moments with a partner.

Now that you have a list of a few two- or a few-word memoirs, could you try to pick which one feels like it's most important or alluring?

It might be helpful to look for patterns across these moments. What do you notice? Are similar people in all these memories? Are the feelings consistent or very different?

CLASSROOM ARTIFACTS

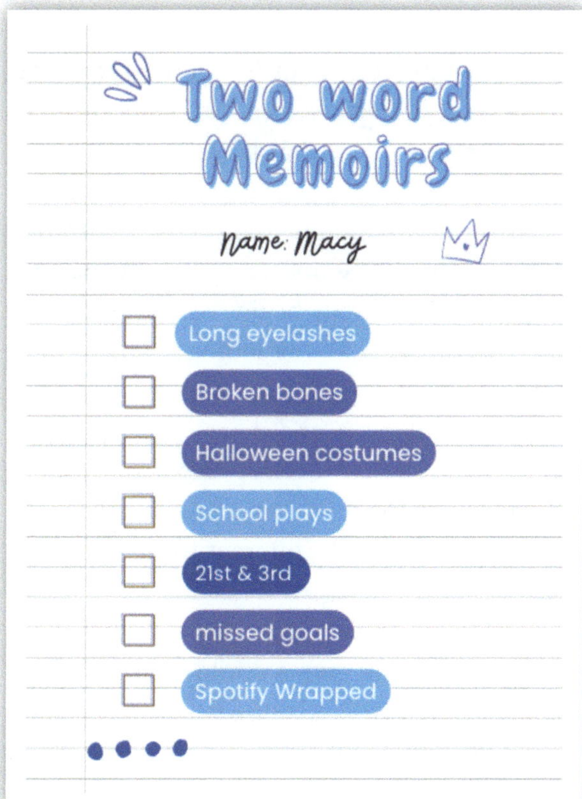

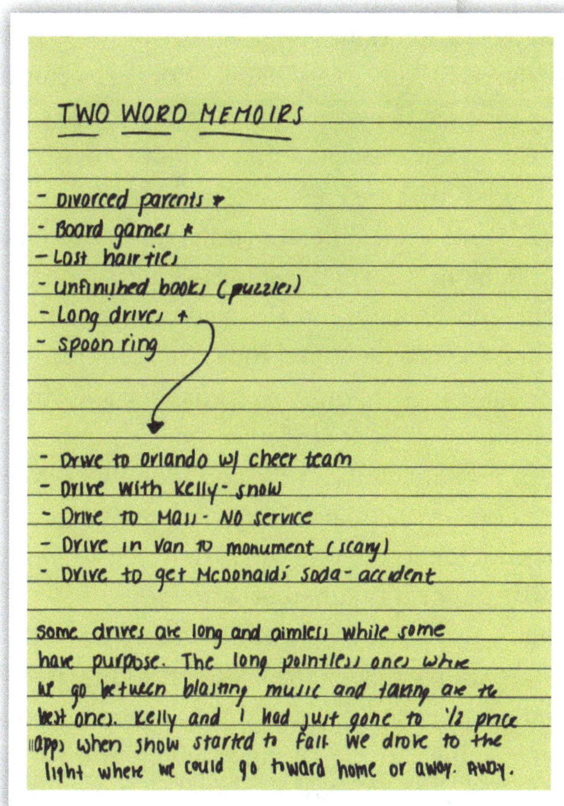

Writers can use two-word memoirs as a way to collect memories that may become a series of vignettes.

Chapter Two: Planning and Drafting with Structure in Mind

Our hope is that your students by now have written some short entries, or freewrites, using some of the strategies for finding their stories from Chapter 1 or other strategies you love. The main thing is recognizing that our best stories rarely arise from our first idea—stories are more skittish and take longer to emerge, which is why it's worth it to try a few different collecting strategies. Now, your writers can choose a story idea (or a series of vignettes) to commit to writing more fully. You'll see that Lesson 1 shares strategies for choosing a story to commit to, and the following lessons are suggestions for planning, including thinking about structure and about parts.

Planning before drafting can help writers raise the level of their first-draft writing. While there is something freeing about spewing words onto a page and figuring out structure and cohesion later, it can also mean that the early draft we produce becomes overwhelming when it comes time to revise. When we consider writing projects that didn't go as well as possible, or that ended up involving a lot of redrafting, we often realize, upon reflection, that we should have spent a little more time planning and preparing to draft.

At the same time, very detailed outlines can make writers anxious about how little room they appear to leave the writer to make discoveries and to innovate. We've also seen students spend so much energy on their plan that it drains energy from their writing. So ... that leaves us looking for ways to plan that are engaging, rapid, and flexible.

You'll find a few different strategies in this chapter that support planning and preparation, from revisiting mentor texts to get ideas for structures, to storyboarding, to working with an AI partner, to verbal rehearsal. You'll also find strategies that support students *as* they begin to draft, including attending to verb tense and time, studying mentor leads, and thinking about endings. Any of these lessons can support your writers as they shift into writing full drafts.

As you coach your students, remember that memoirs can be distinct and diverse in their structures, in how much narrative and how much reflection they include, in whether they focus on one moment or several, in how they play with modalities. Take a moment to revisit some favorite memoirs in anticipation of this work. In doing so, highlight ones that feel quite different from each other that might appeal to different writers.

This is also a good moment to consider which of your students might need extra support. When planning, we try to give the least scaffolding needed, and we try not to give scaffolds to all students that only some students need. You'll see that only one of the lessons that follows includes graphic organizers. Instead, we've suggested a variety of ways that writers might plan, so that your writers can make thoughtful choices about what best matches their intentions and style.

You may also want to revisit and think about modalities with your students—look ahead to Chapter 5, on different modalities students might publish in. If a writer knows they are going to perform their piece as a spoken-word performance, then they might want cuing notes in their memoir, creating more of a prompt/script. If they are going to publish as picture books or graphic novels, they can imagine what information they might share in an image. If a writer wants to include poetry and prose, now is a good time to think about those decisions, as they get ready to draft. Planning and drafting are about looking ahead, knowing that you'll shift some of your decisions as you write.

Lesson 1

Choosing a Story Idea to Fully Draft

STRATEGY

Writers know that their more powerful story ideas often take a while to emerge, which is why they generate a few ideas and freewrite them. Then, they look over this writing, and choose one to fully draft. To make this choice, writers think about which stories they want to commit to more fully.

USE THIS STRATEGY...to help students linger for a moment in the act of choosing their idea, so you can confer with them, so they make thoughtful choices, so that there *is* thought put into this moment.

Visit hs-guidetoteaching.org to access a teaching chart.

TEACH THE STRATEGY

- Suggest to students that it's worth considering which story or stories they want to fully draft as their memoir, and remind them that some memoirs focus on one moment, with reflection woven around or through it, while others tie together a series of vignettes around a central theme or issue.
- Share some strategies for how to make this kind of choice.

When choosing stories to fully draft, writers think about...

- stories for which they have more to say.
- stories they can imagine sharing.
- stories that might offer insight to the writer or their audience.
- stories that reveal hidden themes or issues.
- moments that have troubled or delighted the writer.

- Demonstrate how you might think over some of your story ideas and freewrites, considering which one you might commit to for your memoir, and why.

When Mary did this work with her class, she thought aloud about possibilities, deciding that she had already written enough about when Lisa fed her mud brownies, or when she wanted a Lacoste shirt to fit in with the cool kids. Ultimately, she decided on a track race moment, because she felt it still embodied things she found confusing.

- Invite students to do similar work, spending some time looking over their ideas, what they've jotted, written, and spoken about so far, to choose a story they want to commit to. Suggest that they talk with a partner about this choice.
- End by having writers jot in their notebooks about why they are choosing this story. That reflection will help writers prepare to draft—it often helps them uncover their purpose.

PROMPTS TO COACH STUDENTS AND PARTNERSHIPS

It can be helpful to take a partner on a tour of your notebook, seeing which stories you linger in or which ones feel like you have a lot to say about.

If there's a common thread in your stories, you could write them as a series of vignettes.

If you haven't found the right story yet, it's okay to go back to generating and trying out a few other strategies. You don't always need to be at the same part of the process as your peers.

CLASSROOM ARTIFACTS

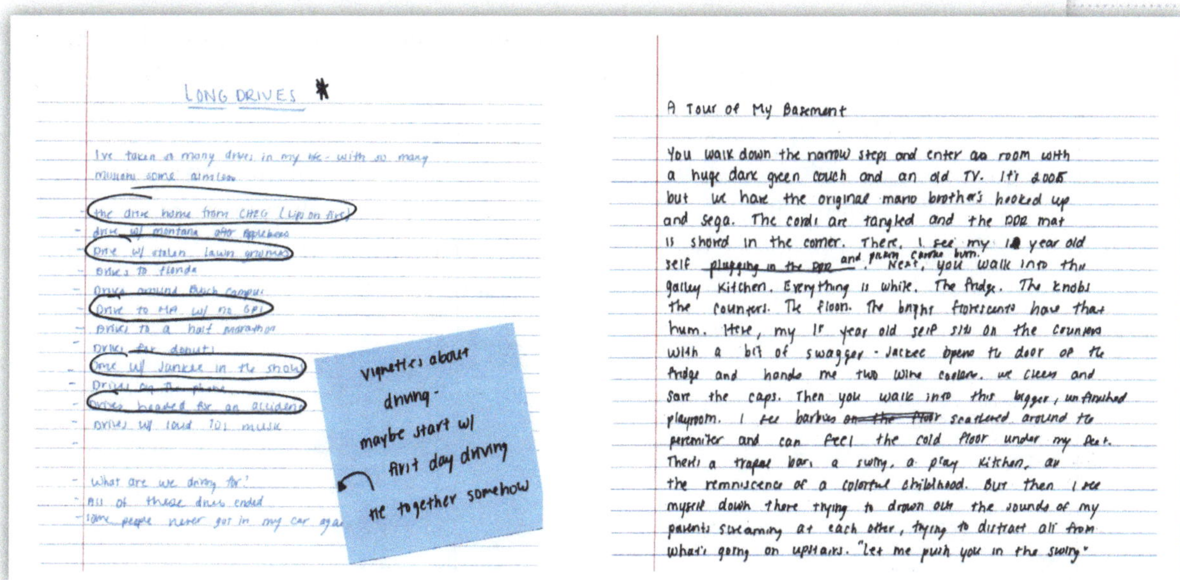

This writer sifts through her notebook entries to decide what she'll write her memoir about.

Lesson 2

Revisiting Mentor Texts for Structure Ideas

STRATEGY

Writers often return to favorite mentor texts as they prepare to write. Often, writers study some favorite texts, asking themselves: How is this text organized? What are the parts of this text? They can also ask themselves: What structural decisions did this writer make that I might also make?

Visit hs-guidetoteaching.org to access a collection of favorite memoirs for teens, as well as this chart on memoir structures.

USE THIS STRATEGY...to help students envision a few different ways they might structure, or organize, their own memoirs.

Inquiry Questions

- How is this text structured - what are the parts of this text?
- What decisions did this writer make about structure that I might also make?

LAUNCH THE INQUIRY

- Suggest to students that immersing oneself in mentor texts can help writers imagine how their own piece might go, especially in terms of structure. Post the inquiry question.
- Engage students in studying one mentor together with you, investigating these inquiry questions. We suggest studying the spoken-word performance "The Bad Haircut" by Alfonso Lacayo, (from *The Moth*, on YouTube) as it is short, engaging, and has a clear structure.

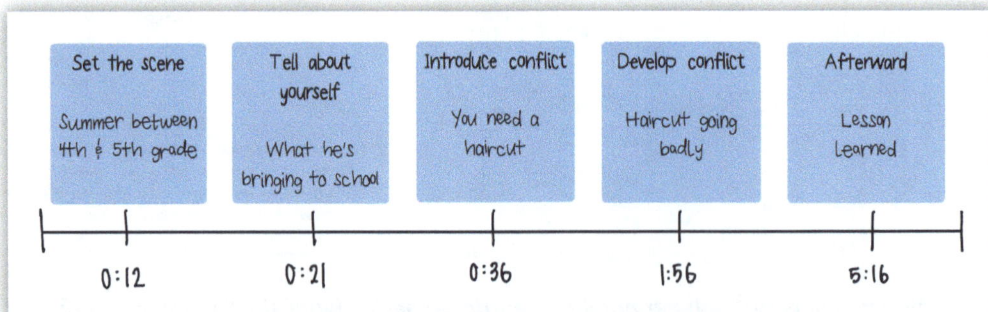

When Lauren did this work with her class, she generated a structural sketch for "The Bad Haircut," noting the distinct parts of Alfonso's narrative and naming these parts as replicable in students' memoirs.

- Alert students that other mentors may have very different structures. Share a chart.
- Make sure students have access to mentor texts, both print and digital, and invite them to revisit some favorites or study new ones, investigating possible structures.
- End with writers talking with a partner about what they've noticed and want to try, and/or jotting one or two possible structures for their own memoir in their notebook.

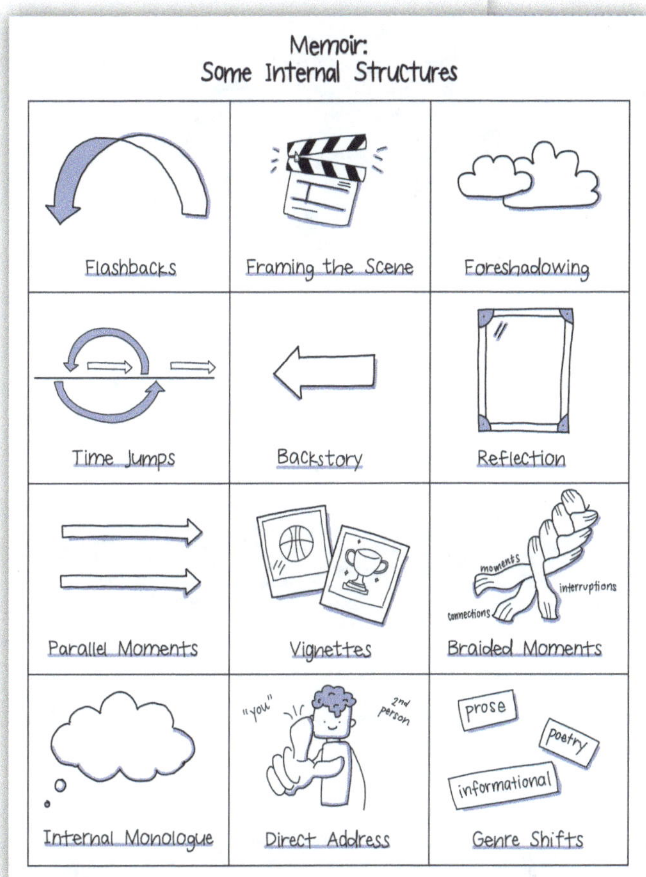

PROMPTS TO COACH STUDENTS AND PARTNERSHIPS

As you study mentors, which structures are you gravitating toward? What are you liking about the way they are organized?

Sometimes what you're really drawn to is a different modality, for the whole memoir or in part. Like maybe you're drawn to poetry and spoken word, for the whole structure or for part.

If you're unsure about structure, one of the easiest structures is to tell your story chronologically, focusing on one moment, and then bookend it with reflection before and after.

CLASSROOM ARTIFACTS

Black Like Me

By Renée Watson

Image to connect to stories

Flashback/ Vignette

When I was in middle school, I was bused to the … y education. Portland Public Schools wanted to integ… Southeast Portland. This meant that a handful of bl… s from Northeast Portland who had attended elementa… …ss town. We together—boarded a yellow school bus before sunrise… sat at the back of the bus laughing at the boys stinging … each other with yo momma jokes. My best friend and I shared the headphones to her Walkman so that we both could sing along to Bell Biv DeVoe and Mariah Carey. For the 30-minute ride we were ourselves and there was no shame in the way we talked or related to each other. No one made a big deal about seeing my hair in braids one day and straightened the next. We bragged about how well our mommas cooked and shared our leftovers with each other at lunchtime, even though one day a white girl loudly whispered to her friend that "black food smells bad."

We had pride and there was a care we took with each other. Though there were normal middle school cliques and dramas, there was also a strength and loyalty among us. On that bus, we …e family. I felt like I belonged.

Transition in place

But when I got to … Which is ironic because I was a plump dark-skinned girl … …k and curl at one drop of rain.

I stood out.

So how is it that I felt no one saw me?

Questions & reflections

Being seen—truly seen—is to feel that all part… …gnized not as compartmentalized pieces of myself, bu… …y identity. So when my white friends told me they didn't see me as a black girl that meant they didn't see me. When white teachers seemed shocked to hear me speak black vernacular in the hallway with my friends when I "spoke so well in class," what they didn't understand is that code-switching came natural to me—I talked both ways and I wasn't trying to fit in with my friends or impress my teachers. I was being myself.

Vignette

One day, on our way to a field trip to… …phony, a teacher tried to assure me that if I "gave the … …ally find that I liked it. I told her that I loved classical mus… …o. Her smile told me that she thought this was a good t… "Well, that's good because that rap stuff is not music," I t… …-hop and R&B and gospel and country, too. My family … …amily. We had a collection of records that included Tennessee Ernie Ford, Mahalia Jackson,

"Oh, that's right," my teacher said. "You got an A." She turned her back to me and addressed the rest of the class. "And this is why I am so disappointed in all of you. You let Renée Watson come all the way over here from Northeast Portland and get a better grade than you in science!"

Hypotheticals & what-ifs

I have often replayed that day in my mind. I have thought of new endings where I stand up for myself and walk out of class refusing to be humiliated. I have wondered what would have happened if she asked me to h… for the other students in class. What if she taught me— class—about black scientists and their revolutionar… she had allowed space in her narrative for black children… nd to be capable of meeting high expectations, of achie… s?

What if she really saw me?

Question as transition

As an educator, I try … encourage them to embrace all parts of their culture… …om, what they eat, the music they enjoy, the joyous ar… …heir neighborhoods and families. I strive to learn their … …ve histories. I share my stories with them, and we grow… …e laugh at ourselves for sometimes being the stereotype. We proudly … …m that we are more than the stereotype. We mourn and rejoice over our ancestors—their struggles and victories, their shortcomings and strengths. We commit … our true selves. We commit to seeing each other.

Present-day story

black like me

and suddenly everyone would see

how black i am.

Repetition

black like collard greens & salted meat simmering o…
black like hot water cornbread & iron skillets, like juk…
black like soul train lines & the electric slide at weddi…
black like vaseline on ashy knees, like beads decorat…
black like cotton fields & soul-cried spirituals.

my skin is black

like red kool-aid, red soda, the red blood
of the lynched and assassinated and the african man
those skinheads killed with a baseball bat when i w… in the fifth grade.

Poetry

i am as black as he was.
my science teacher knows this. she sees
my black and is blind to my brilliance.
can't believe i passed the test with an a
when all the white kids failed.

and when she says to the white students,
"you ought to be ashamed of yourselves . . ."
what she really wants to say is, "i can't believe this black girl is as smart as you."

Referencing school stories from earlier section

all the white kids look at me
and this is when we learn that the color of our shells
come with expectations.

i stop being good
at science and math.

my english teacher gives me books and journals
and i read and write the world
as it is, as i want it to be.
i read past my black blues, discover that i am black
like benjamin banneker and george washington carver
black like margaret walker and fannie lou hamer

Annotating Renée Watson's "Black Like Me" for structural moves.

Playing with Time

Lesson 3

STRATEGY

Memoir writers often play with time, sometimes starting ahead or behind their central moment, sometimes linking several vignettes, not necessarily chronologically. Often, it can be helpful to jot a timeline and move different sticky notes or points around on it as a way to plan how a memoir might go.

USE THIS STRATEGY...to support students in planning the parts of their memoir and how they will move the reader through time across these parts. This strategy especially helps writers make decisions about chronology, before they start writing.

TEACH THE STRATEGY

- Suggest to students that memoirists often play with time, making decisions about where their story will start, if it will move backward or forward in time, or both.
- Demonstrate how you might jot a timeline of possible moments/parts of your memoir, voicing over as you move a moment forward or back in time.

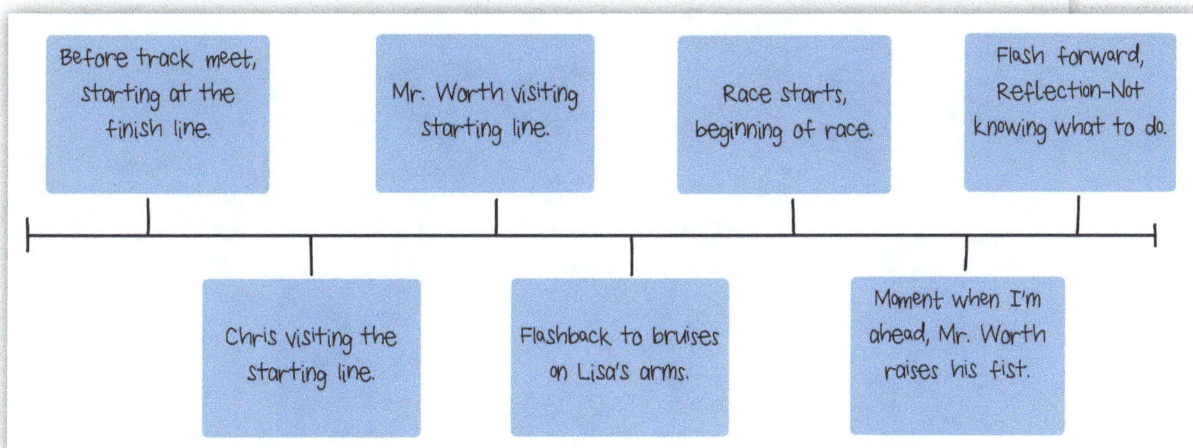

When Mary demonstrated this strategy, she jotted a timeline for the memoir piece she was planning to draft alongside her students. As she spoke, she played with moving parts around, such as putting the reflection first, and then the whole piece being a flashback, or putting the reflection at the end, as a kind of resolution.

- Invite students to look over the writing and jotting they did when they were collecting ideas and possible moments and to play with possible timelines for their own memoirs. Encourage students to first jot, and then to share their thinking with a partner.

PROMPTS TO COACH STUDENTS AND PARTNERSHIPS

Some memoirs focus on one moment, and they surround that moment with reflection before and after, or just before or after. That might work for you.

Sometimes writers have several moments they want to string together. If you want, you can try out different orders, playing with chronology. You might, for instance, try starting with the earliest moment, and go forward in time, and then try a different order, to see what you like best.

Occasionally a memoir is all story, all one moment, and so it's only the narrator's in-the-moment inner thinking that offers insights and realizations—that might work for you.

CLASSROOM ARTIFACTS

Coley creates two different storyboards for her memoir.

Turning to AI for Structure Possibilities

Lesson 4

STRATEGY

Writers often find that asking an AI partner for advice about structure can be really helpful. They give their AI partner information about their story and ask for multiple ideas.

USE THIS STRATEGY...to help your writers imagine various structure possibilities and increase their adeptness with AI as a thought partner.

Visit hs-guidetoteaching.org to access a chart of tips for prompting AI for structure possibilities.

TEACH THE STRATEGY

- Suggest to students that AI can be a helpful partner in expanding writers' ideas about structure. Share the chart and talk through tips for prompting an AI partner.
- Demonstrate prompting an AI partner for structure options, as shown in the Classroom Artifacts on the right.
- Share the structure options AI suggested, demonstrating your thoughts on each one, and how you blend them or build off the options.
- Invite your students to consider the suggestions your AI partner makes, along with you, and consider if you might choose one of these suggestions, adapt one, or mix and match.
- Set up your students to do similar work, suggesting they work with a partner to get help prompting their AI partner, if needed (or set up your EdTech to directly invite students to begin this work).

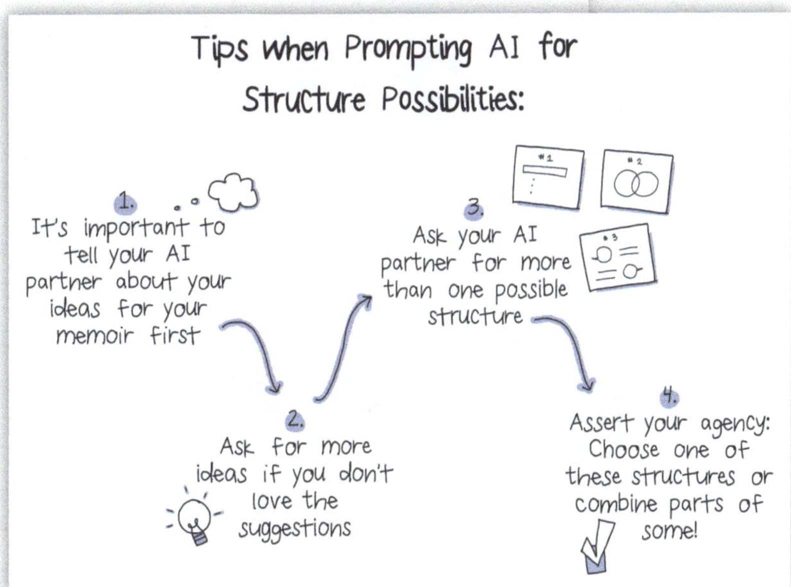

PROMPTS TO COACH STUDENTS AND PARTNERSHIPS

Remember to first tell your AI partner about your ideas for your memoir. Give it plenty of information to work with.

It helps to tell AI about possible parts you're considering. Don't worry about what order they'll go—your AI partner can help with that.

Always ask for multiple suggestions, and if you don't love any of the structures, tell your AI partner that, and ask for more suggestions.

CLASSROOM ARTIFACTS

I'm getting ready to draft a memoir. It's about a moment, in my senior year of high school, when I made the national track competition in hurdles. I ended up competing against my best friend, Lisa. The race had scholarships attached to it, for college, which we both wanted. My boyfriend was also at the race - Chris. He had briefly dated Lisa when we were younger. About a year before, Lisa's mother had died, and she lived with her father and younger brother. Her father often seemed angry, and I remember one day when Lisa came to school with bruises on her arms, that she wouldn't talk about. During the race, I got to this one moment when I was ahead of Lisa, and I saw her father, raising his fist in the stands. I didn't know whether to keep trying to win. Can you help me imagine two different possible structures for this memoir?

Mary gave her AI partner plenty of information to work with, including details about her life at that time, her interests, and her preoccupations.

1. Braided Structure (Interwoven Threads)

This structure would weave together multiple storylines—your friendship with Lisa, the pressures of the race, and the deeper context of Lisa's home life—allowing each thread to build toward the climactic moment on the track.

- **Opening Scene:** Begin in the **middle of the race**, right at the moment when you see Lisa's father raising his fist. Freeze the action for a second, holding the tension.
- **First Thread (Backstory on Friendship & Rivalry):** Flashback to how you and Lisa became friends, your shared love for track, and the ways competition shaped your relationship.
- **Second Thread (Lisa's Home Life):** Introduce details about Lisa's mother's death, her father's anger, and the bruises you once noticed but never spoke about.
- **Third Thread (Your Own Motivations):** Reflect on your own ambitions, the scholarship, your boyfriend Chris, and the emotions that make this race so loaded.
- **Return to the Race (Climax):** Unfreeze the moment on the track—what do you decide? Do you push forward? Do you hesitate? Do you think about Lisa's future? End with the outcome.
- **Reflection (Ending):** Explore what that moment meant in retrospect. Did it shape how you saw competition, ambition, or friendship? What would you say to your younger self now?

2. Framing Device (Present-to-Past Reflection)

This structure would start with you as an adult—perhaps reflecting on the race from a distance—before diving back into the experience in real-time.

- **Opening Scene (Present Day):** Start with a moment in adulthood—maybe watching a track race on TV or at your own child's event—where something reminds you of that pivotal race.
- **Flashback to Senior Year:** Shift into the past, telling the story from the perspective of your younger self, leading up to the race.
- **Slow-Build Tension:** Introduce key moments—training, conversations with Lisa, seeing Chris at the event, thinking about the scholarship and what it means for your future.
- **Race Sequence (Real-Time Storytelling):** Describe the race as it happens, heartbeat by heartbeat, hurdle by hurdle, leading to the exact moment of hesitation.
- **Aftermath:** Return to the present—how did that moment impact you? What happened to Lisa? How does the memory sit with you now?

Mary's AI partner suggested two possible structure ideas.

Verbal Rehearsal as a Drafting Tool

Lesson 5

STRATEGY

Experienced writers know that one of the best ways to plan their piece is to say their story out loud. Sometimes specific verbal cues can help a writer shift from one part of a memoir to another or try parts of their piece in different ways.

USE THIS STRATEGY... to support students in preparing to draft. Oral rehearsal helps writers develop more fluency, hear where they have gaps in their piece, and get feedback. Verbal cues help writers imagine transitions.

Visit hs-guidetoteaching.org to access a collection of printable cue cards for verbal rehearsal.

TEACH THE STRATEGY

- Suggest to students that one of the best ways to rehearse writing is through verbal rehearsal. Add that cue cards help speakers find more to say and that partners can prompt each other with cue cards.
- Gather your plan (it might be a timeline, storyboard, or sticky notes), and demonstrate how you will point to each part, and say that part of your piece out loud. Introduce the Verbal Cues for Memoir cards.

Verbal Cues for Memoir

I remember the moment when...	It all started...	When I think about...I think about the time when...
When I think about this now, I realize/wonder...	Sometimes you don't realize the significance of a moment until later. For me...	Picture this...
It was only much later that I thought about...	Now imagine that it's...later...and...	Long before this...
Later I found myself thinking/feeling/in a similar experience...	On the outside, I... But on the inside I...	Even afterward, I remained unsure of...

Lesson 5 (Continued)

- Select a student to act as your partner, and demonstrate how you might begin by saying the beginning of your memoir, and then after saying a bit, your partner can choose another card, prompting you to say more. You can also lay out a few cards you think could work for your piece.
- Invite students to do similar work with their partners. They might return to their plan, choose the cards they think will work for them, and rehearse this way. Or, they might let their partner choose different cards, to see if these prompts lead them in interesting directions. After students talk through ideas using these prompts, they should do some jotting to capture their thinking. Or students can video-record themselves as they speak.

PROMPTS TO COACH STUDENTS AND PARTNERSHIPS

Sometimes you know how your memoir will go, and you can simply use some verbal cues if they help you transition from part to part.

Sometimes these verbal cues will help you try out some reflection, or help you shift between parts of your memoir.

These cues are not just to help you say more, they are to help you write more. You can use these as writing prompts, too!

CLASSROOM ARTIFACTS

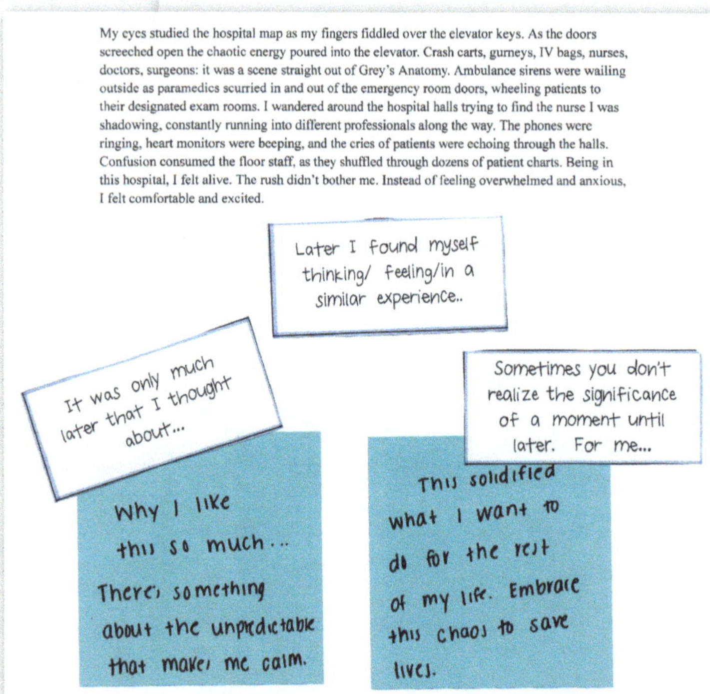

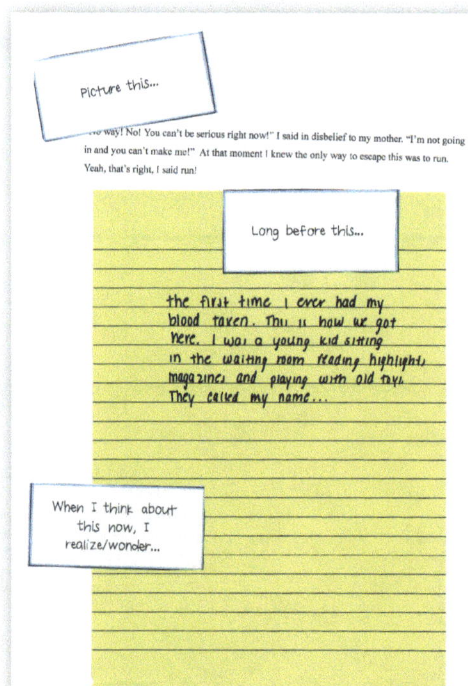

Verbal rehearsal cards help writers find more to say and imagine the parts of their memoir.

Extracting What You're Really Trying to Say

Lesson 6

STRATEGY

Memorists know that sometimes they want to reveal more explicitly what their story is really about. To get at this knowledge, they ask themselves questions and try to create a more intentionally angled draft.

USE THIS STRATEGY...to support students in figuring out the purpose and meaning of their story. This is especially important in a genre like memoir where stories usually have something deeper bubbling below the surface, such as a hidden theme or issue.

Visit hs-guidetoteaching.org to access this teaching chart on extracting deeper meanings in memoir.

TEACH THE STRATEGY

- Suggest to students that because memoir authors are inevitably writing about their own life, they know all the little secrets about their story, but their reader might need these meanings to be more explicit. Explain that memoirists try to extract what they are really trying to say in their story and work to make that explicit.
- Study a memoir with students, asking them what the story is really about. We suggest "Cheetah" from Glennon Doyle's *Untamed* (2020), or the picture book *A Different Pond* by Bao Phi and Thi Bui (2017), but most memoirs or excerpts will work. Together, generate a few different possibilities around what the story is really about.
- Demonstrate this work of excavating meaning with your own writing, looking at your freewriting or a first draft, trying to figure out what it's about.

Lesson 6 (Continued)

- Model two different ways your memoir might go, depending on the purpose you want to lean into.

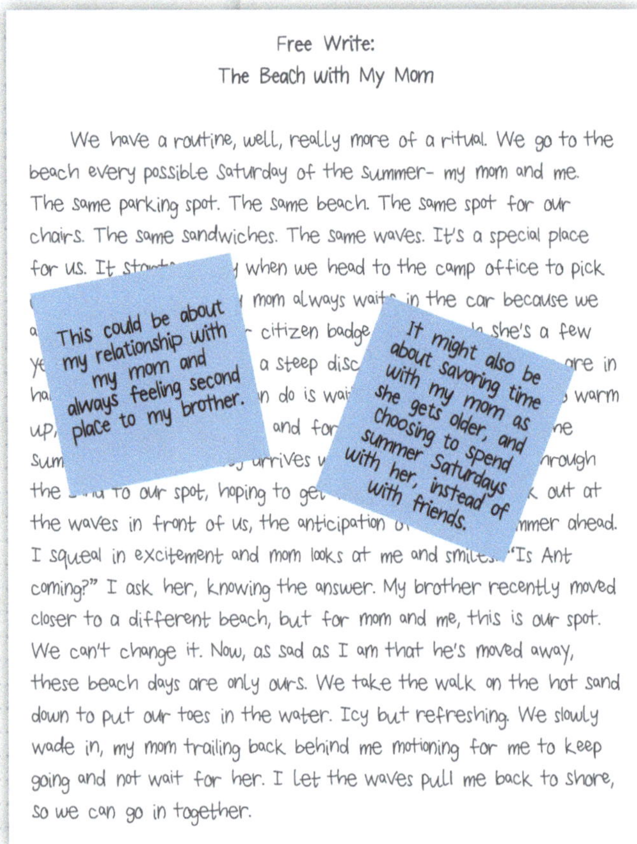

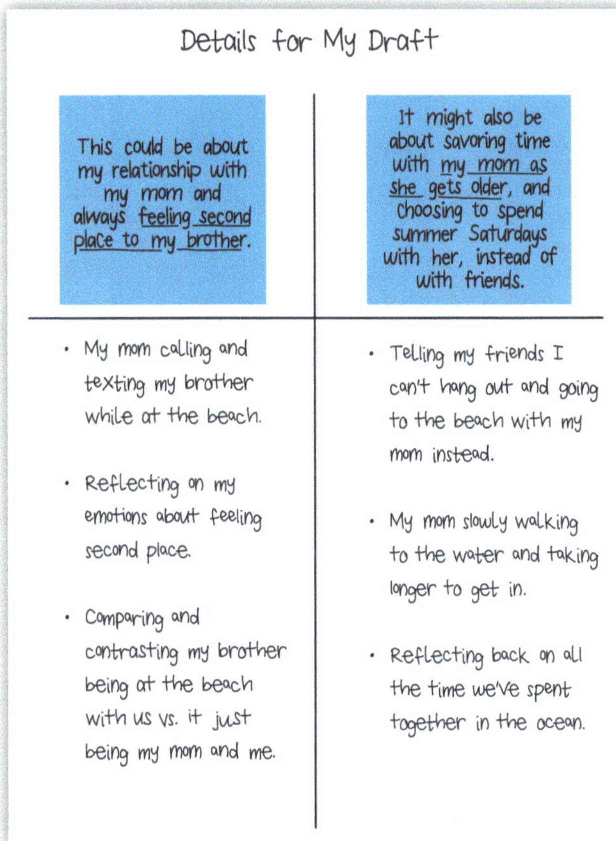

As Coley modeled this strategy with a class, she displayed her freewrite, recognizing that the big topics were both about the beach and her mom. As she studied the content, she thought aloud about what she might be trying to say about each of these topics and jotted that on sticky notes. Then, she moved the sticky notes to a new sheet and brainstormed details she could include to bring out the deeper meaning for each topic.

- Offer the chart to students as they try this work of looking at their own memoir topics and freewrites.
- Support students as they:
  - think through what they are really trying to say in their stories
  - angle their narratives based on their purpose (talking and/or freewriting ideas)
  - draft their pieces or redraft parts

PROMPTS TO COACH STUDENTS AND PARTNERSHIPS

How might you tell your story differently if ______ is the purpose? Does it change any details you want to add or the starting place? Or maybe the ending?

Remember, our memoirs don't necessarily need conflicts to be about something super dramatic. Consider what you are really saying about your identity or a relationship or a certain emotion.

Try leaning on a trusted writing partner here, asking them what they think your story might really be about. Sometimes they can see something you're not necessarily seeing.

CLASSROOM ARTIFACTS

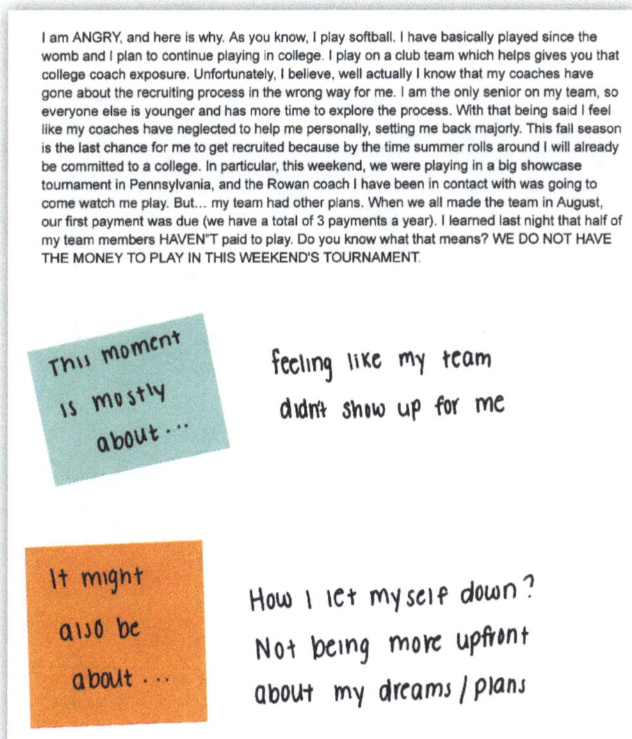
I am ANGRY, and here is why. As you know, I play softball. I have basically played since the womb and I plan to continue playing in college. I play on a club team which helps gives you that college coach exposure. Unfortunately, I believe, well actually I know that my coaches have gone about the recruiting process in the wrong way for me. I am the only senior on my team, so everyone else is younger and has more time to explore the process. With that being said I feel like my coaches have neglected to help me personally, setting me back majorly. This fall season is the last chance for me to get recruited because by the time summer rolls around I will already be committed to a college. In particular, this weekend, we were playing in a big showcase tournament in Pennsylvania, and the Rowan coach I have been in contact with was going to come watch me play. But… my team had other plans. When we all made the team in August, our first payment was due (we have a total of 3 payments a year). I learned last night that half of my team members HAVEN"T paid to play. Do you know what that means? WE DO NOT HAVE THE MONEY TO PLAY IN THIS WEEKEND'S TOURNAMENT.

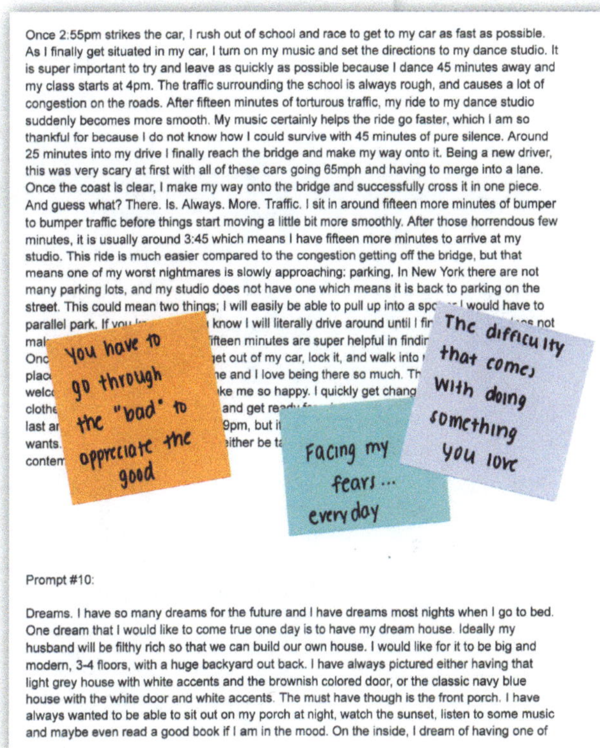
Once 2:55pm strikes the car, I rush out of school and race to get to my car as fast as possible. As I finally get situated in my car, I turn on my music and set the directions to my dance studio. It is super important to try and leave as quickly as possible because I dance 45 minutes away and my class starts at 4pm. The traffic surrounding the school is always rough, and causes a lot of congestion on the roads. After fifteen minutes of torturous traffic, my ride to my dance studio suddenly becomes more smooth. My music certainly helps the ride go faster, which I am so thankful for because I do not know how I could survive with 45 minutes of pure silence. Around 25 minutes into my drive I finally reach the bridge and make my way onto it. Being a new driver, this was very scary at first with all of these cars going 65mph and having to merge into a lane. Once the coast is clear, I make my way onto the bridge and successfully cross it in one piece. And guess what? There. Is. Always. More. Traffic. I sit in around fifteen more minutes of bumper to bumper traffic before things start moving a little bit more smoothly. After those horrendous few minutes, it is usually around 3:45 which means I have fifteen more minutes to arrive at my studio. This ride is much easier compared to the congestion getting off the bridge, but that means one of my worst nightmares is slowly approaching: parking. In New York there are not many parking lots, and my studio does not have one which means it is back to parking on the street. This could mean two things; I will easily be able to pull up into a spo… I would have to parallel park. …

Prompt #10:

Dreams. I have so many dreams for the future and I have dreams most nights when I go to bed. One dream that I would like to come true one day is to have my dream house. Ideally my husband will be filthy rich so that we can build our own house. I would like for it to be big and modern, 3-4 floors, with a huge backyard out back. I have always pictured either having that light grey house with white accents and the brownish colored door, or the classic navy blue house with the white door and white accents. The must have though is the front porch. I have always wanted to be able to sit out on my porch at night, watch the sunset, listen to some music and maybe even read a good book if I am in the mood. On the inside, I dream of having one of

Finding hidden issues and themes inside one's story.

Lesson 7

Returning to Mentors to Study Beginnings

STRATEGY

Writers study mentors across the writing process. One especially helpful moment for memoirists to return to mentors is when they are ready to write (or revise) beginnings. Then, they can revisit favorite mentors, asking what these other memoirists have done to set the scene or launch the reader into the memoir.

Visit hs-guidetoteaching.org to download a collection of memoir leads.

USE THIS STRATEGY...to help writers start their drafts at a higher level and to inculcate a personal writing process that includes working with mentor texts in a variety of ways across the writing process.

Inquiry Questions

- What can I learn about the art of beginnings, by studying the work of other writers?
- What do these other writers do that I might want to try?

LAUNCH THE INQUIRY

- Suggest to students that writers often try the beginnings of their pieces more than one way, as the beginning launches their reader into their story. Add that one way to get ideas for different ways to start is to study mentors. Post the inquiry question.
- Invite students to join you in studying two sample beginnings and to collect moves memoir writers make (literary techniques) that students could mimic. We suggest "A Bad Haircut" by Alonso Lacayo, "Run" by Trevor Noah, or "Saint of Dry Creek" by Patrick Haggerty, but of course, return to your favorites.
- Gather some of these techniques into an informal chart.
- Invite students to study favorite mentors, paying particular attention to their beginnings, and to add to this collection of moves.

- Then invite students to draft or revise one or two versions of the beginning of their memoir and to share with a partner, talking about what they were inspired by, and what they tried.

Techniques Writers Use at the Beginning of Memoirs...

- Give specific details of place, time
- Hint at upcoming trouble
- Introduce characters
- Start with dialogue or authentic voice
- Alternate between a "now" voice & a "then" voice
- Begin with a moment of reflection
- Start with a dramatic moment
- Introduce groups, culture, history, or social issues that matter
- Offer backstory

PROMPTS TO COACH STUDENTS AND PARTNERSHIPS

It's always great to go back to a memoir you liked and see what that writer did, because you probably already like their style.

Often writers try two, three, or even more different beginnings, as a way to experiment.

A lot of memoir writers give very specific details at the start—how old they were, where they were—that help orient the reader.

CLASSROOM ARTIFACTS

"Picture Day"

I'm marching home from school in my khaki shorts, a buttoned down shirt and my "fancy" shoes. It's mid-September, the perfect time of year. But it's also the day, my brother and our friends informed me that it was picture day. And regretfully I believed them.

This writer inserts some foreshadowing into their beginning.

The Epitome of the Man vs Self Conflict

Footsteps, someone blowing their nose, pen clicking, whispering, pages being flipped, the sound of a chair being adjusted, crinkling plastic water bottles, color of the lights, direction of the lights, temperature, my cold hands, melody of the teacher's voice, the sound of pencil writing on paper or dropping to the floor, the sound of typing, my unsharpened pencil, my runny nose, the urge to tap on my desk, or cough. Why couldn't I just focus on my work?

I remember the first time I learned that I have ADHD.

This writer creates a vivid image, followed by a revelatory question.

Lesson 8

Drafting with Time (and Verb Tense) in Mind

STRATEGY

Writers make deliberate decisions about verb tenses to convey relationships between actions, reflection, and time. Past tense often creates a sense of reflectiveness, while present tense can increase the immediacy. One strategy worth trying is to experiment with tenses before drafting a whole piece, or as a way to revise.

Visit hs-guidetoteaching.org to download a chart of verb tenses and their relationship to action and time.

USE THIS STRATEGY... to encourage experimentation and choice early in the writing process. You can also make this strategy more complex by introducing more sophisticated verb tenses such as past perfect, to convey sequence, relationships, and shifts in action and time.

TEACH THE STRATEGY

- Introduce the idea that writers make deliberate decisions about verb tenses as they start their pieces. Sometimes they have purposeful decisions in mind; other times they try their piece more than one way, to see which they like better.
- Demonstrate how you might start your memoir, starting it with the same language but two different verb tenses. Invite students to talk to a partner about which they prefer and why.

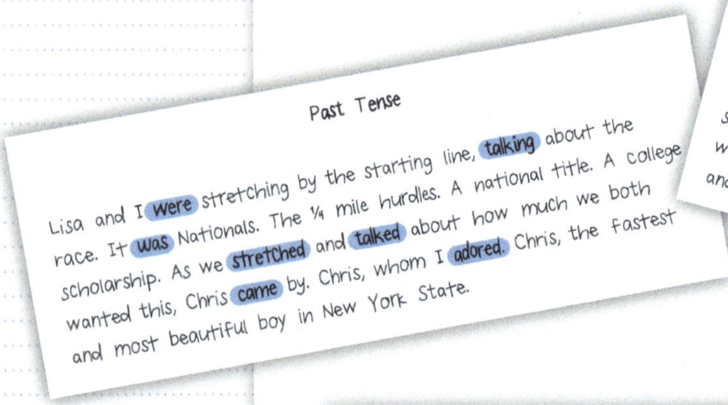

Past Tense

Lisa and I were stretching by the starting line, talking about the race. It was Nationals. The ¼ mile hurdles. A national title. A college scholarship. As we stretched and talked about how much we both wanted this, Chris came by. Chris, whom I adored. Chris, the fastest and most beautiful boy in New York State.

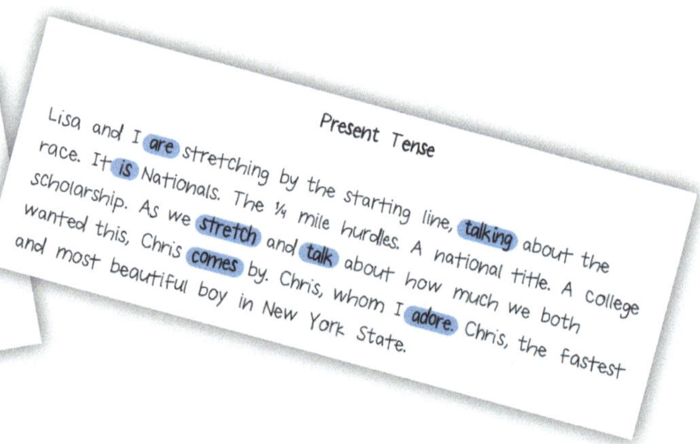

Present Tense

Lisa and I are stretching by the starting line, talking about the race. It is Nationals. The ¼ mile hurdles. A national title. A college scholarship. As we stretch and talk about how much we both wanted this, Chris comes by. Chris, whom I adore. Chris, the fastest and most beautiful boy in New York State.

When Mary demonstrated, she shared the first few lines of her memoir and read them aloud two different ways, emphasizing the different tones of the tenses. Then she invited students to talk with a partner about which they preferred for her memoir, and why. It's always going to be worth it to teach students to make choices, rather than follow directions.

- Invite students to do similar work—to draft and/or say the very beginning of their memoir in two different tenses. Often, students need to write it to focus on the verb tenses.
- If they are ready to draft, students can then go on to drafting, knowing they can think about tenses across their drafts.

PROMPTS TO COACH STUDENTS AND PARTNERSHIPS

It often helps to write the first paragraph two ways, so you can really focus on finding the verbs and changing the tenses.

If you have dialogue, your dialogue will almost always be in the present tense, even if your narration is in the past.

It can be interesting to play with other forms of past tense, to show the different moments.

CLASSROOM ARTIFACTS

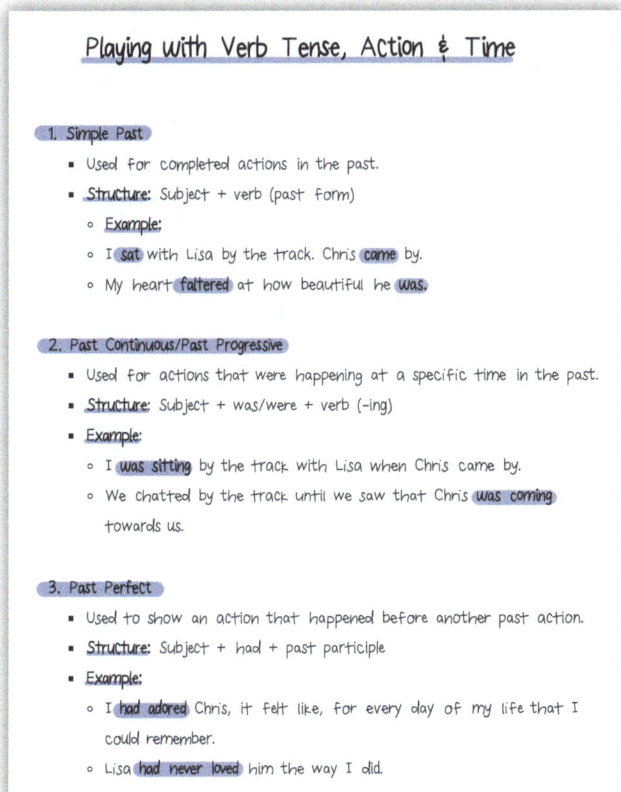

Playing with Verb Tense, Action & Time

1. Simple Past
   - Used for completed actions in the past.
   - Structure: Subject + verb (past form)
     - Example:
     - I sat with Lisa by the track. Chris came by.
     - My heart faltered at how beautiful he was.

2. Past Continuous/Past Progressive
   - Used for actions that were happening at a specific time in the past.
   - Structure: Subject + was/were + verb (-ing)
   - Example:
     - I was sitting by the track with Lisa when Chris came by.
     - We chatted by the track until we saw that Chris was coming towards us.

3. Past Perfect
   - Used to show an action that happened before another past action.
   - Structure: Subject + had + past participle
   - Example:
     - I had adored Chris, it felt like, for every day of my life that I could remember.
     - Lisa had never loved him the way I did.

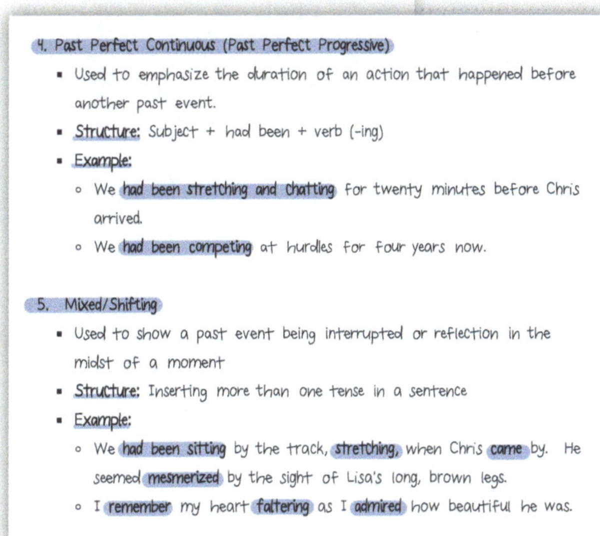

4. Past Perfect Continuous (Past Perfect Progressive)
   - Used to emphasize the duration of an action that happened before another past event.
   - Structure: Subject + had been + verb (-ing)
   - Example:
     - We had been stretching and chatting for twenty minutes before Chris arrived.
     - We had been competing at hurdles for four years now.

5. Mixed/Shifting
   - Used to show a past event being interrupted or reflection in the midst of a moment
   - Structure: Inserting more than one tense in a sentence
   - Example:
     - We had been sitting by the track, stretching, when Chris came by. He seemed mesmerized by the sight of Lisa's long, brown legs.
     - I remember my heart faltering as I admired how beautiful he was.

Often students need vocabulary for describing possible verb tenses.

Lesson 9

The Purpose and Craft of Memoir Endings

STRATEGY

Memoir writers take their endings as seriously as their beginnings, knowing that last words often stay with a reader. They often consider different kinds of endings, including ones that suggest realizations, insights, lessons, and/or possible change, and they convey these with either expository writing or literary craft.

Visit hs-guidetoteaching.org to access a chart on purposes and craft of memoir endings.

USE THIS STRATEGY...to help writers achieve a sense of closure and/or to support writers in reflecting on their story.

TEACH THE STRATEGY

- Suggest to your writers that endings are as important as beginnings and that writers often consider different kinds of endings.
- Share a chart of memoir endings and talk a bit about the different purposes of these endings.

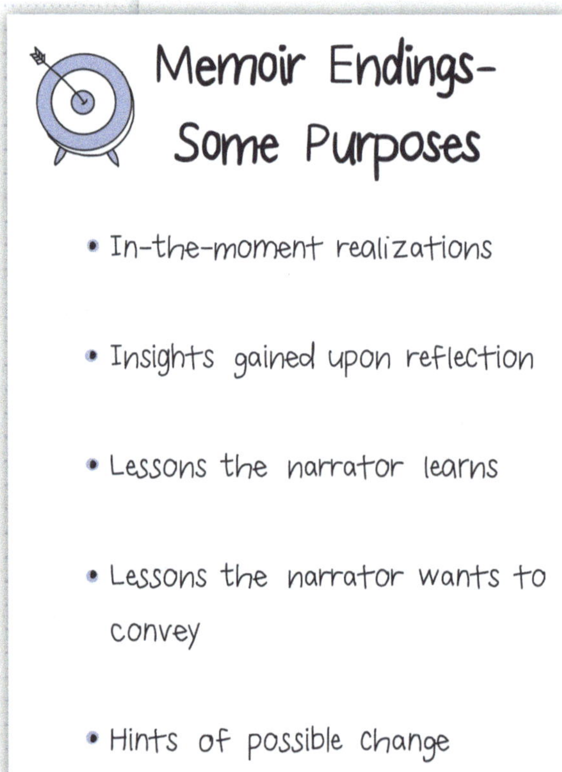

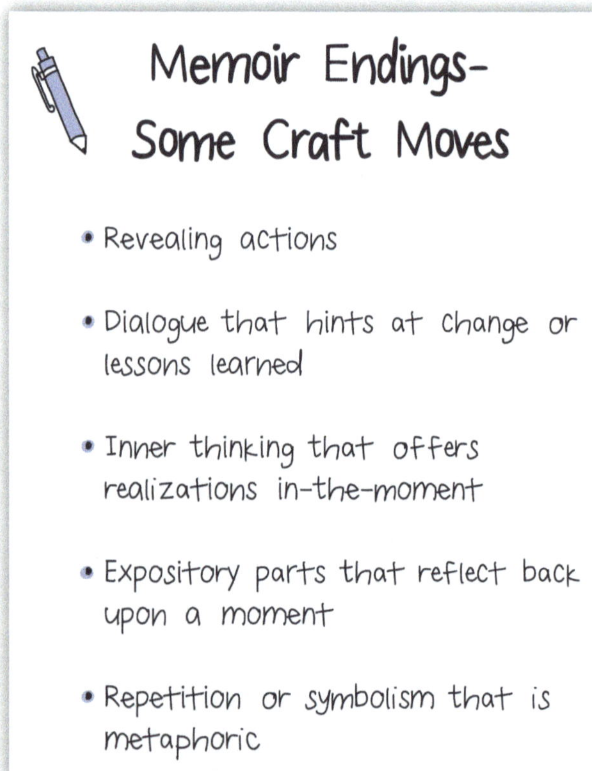

- Explain that memoir writers not only decide what they want to accomplish with their endings, they also think about how their ending will go—what craft moves they'll use. Share, or cocreate, another chart naming craft moves for endings.
- Demonstrate how you might try an ending for your memoir two different ways (or share this mentor), and invite students to compare the purposes and craft of each.

Ending #1

After the race, Chris came up and put his arm around me. "You did it, Mary," he whispered, pulling my ponytail gently. Then, even lower, "and I know why. I get it."

We both looked over at Lisa, standing next to her dad, who was praising her, his big hands gentle on her back as he hugged her.

My family didn't get it. My coach didn't get it. But Chris did, and Lisa did, and that was enough.

Ending #2

When I think about this race now, it's hard for me to remember anything except confusion and fear. Fear that I didn't understand what was happening to Lisa, fear that I might let my family down by losing and my friend down by winning, and confusion over how this race had come to be about so much more than running fast. I know it felt as if those single seconds were lasting hours, and that no decision I made would make everyone, or maybe anyone, happy.

Ultimately, I put friendship above all else. I regretted it, a little, at the awards dinner, and when my brother was extra kind because I lost. But I was never sorry, really.

When Mary did this work with her class, she showed two different endings for her memoir, one expository and one narrative, and invited students to consider which they liked best for her memoir, and why, and which might work better for theirs.

- Invite students to try this out for their own memoirs, drafting their ending in an expository and a narrative way, trying different purposes and craft.

PROMPTS TO COACH STUDENTS AND PARTNERSHIPS

It's often helpful to try two endings. You might try two different purposes, or try one as expository and one as narrative. Sometimes you come to new insights.

When you're unsure, it helps to simply start, "When I think about this now ..." and see what comes out.

You don't have to hit your reader over the head with an explicit lesson. It's okay to hint at a partial realization or suggest that something began to change.

CLASSROOM ARTIFACTS

Ending #1

In the end, I have realized that life is the sum of challenges overcome. Everyone has a unique cross to bear, a time when they may ask "why me?" Whether it's personal trauma or suffering, mental health, or monetary issues, there are difficulties that must be accepted and conquered in order to attain peace. Mine is my accident. And although I recognize its importance in my life, my mentality towards it has shifted. I no longer feel short-changed. I am bigger than any misfortunate that comes at me. It does not need to define who I am and I do not need to give it lasting control and power over me. I too am the master of my fate and the captain of my soul.

These writers play with endings that capture lessons, offer closure, or suggest change.

Ending #2

There is a lure, a unique beauty, to playing baseball in a land of soccer. There is a magic that slowly and subtly grows, bubbles, and eventually boils over, when you share eight years of your life, week after week, with the same group of kids. Hours every week, practices, every weekend given to this game. Almost everyone on the team comes from a culture whose lifeblood is this sport. It's hard work, all the time, and it's an escape, too; baseball is a constant in a world where everything else changes continuously. When life gets overwhelming, it is astoundingly liberating to be surrounded by teammates different in background but united by a game we love.

These writers play with endings that capture lessons, offer closure, or suggest change.

Chapter Three: Revising with the Lenses of Craft and Elaboration

Writer and writing teacher Roy Peter Clark calls the draft "your ticket to the revision party" (2012). He suggests that the real fun, and the real work, happens once you've got a draft in play. We believe that. You improve at soccer when you get on the field; you get better at piano when you put your fingers on the keyboard. We also love how thinking of revision as a writing party makes writing feel less intimidating.

The lessons in this chapter are dedicated to helping students raise the level of their memoirs. These lessons also aim to instill skills that will help your students become more powerful writers overall, by coaching them to think about the effect they want to achieve and techniques writers use to achieve that effect. A lot of young writers tend to think about what they want to write about, but less about *how* they'll write. In these lessons, you can choose among a variety of craft and elaboration techniques that will serve your young writers well across genres. Narrative craft infuses nonfiction as well as fiction writing.

You'll notice that several of the lessons invite your writers to study mentor texts—either from published writers or teacher-written demonstration texts—and investigate the moves these writers make that they might also try. It's always worth it to instill this habit of returning to mentor texts across the writing process, as it will support your writers long after they have left your classroom. Also, when students study mentors, they'll notice multiple techniques, which give them more to experiment with than just a single strategy for elaboration. Lesson 1, for instance, which leads your students to investigate many techniques that memoir writers use, is one that they can return to in order to study any particular part of their memoir they are considering revising.

To be a memoir, a piece must have a story at its heart, so most of these lessons focus on developing narrative craft. But memoir also has reflective and expository parts. And it can be poetic, either in its language and imagery, or literally, in whole or in parts. You'll see lessons that develop these aspects of memoir as well.

As students pursue this kind of revision, it's helpful for them to have the same writing partner, so that partner can be a coach, a reader, a celebrant. If you set up your students with EdTech AI partners, make sure they save these chats, so their AI partner can also give them feedback over time and help your writers see the ways they are growing. We do recommend that students have EdTech AI partners, as otherwise they will seek to work with ChatGPT or another open AI outside of class, and you won't be able to advise them or shape those interactions.

With memoir, as with any genre, it's important to have students reflect on their choices as writers and on their revisions. Why did you move that section here? How does this word help build the mood? How did it feel to start the introduction with dialogue instead of with the setting? Questions like these help writers recognize their choices are intentional and serve a purpose aligned with the content of their writing.

The goal, of course, in all of this, is to make revision a party—a party where writers feel excited at the prospect of lifting the level of their memoir and ready for the challenge that comes with micro and macro revision. Just as you model how to add dialogue or how to stretch out a scene, you can model this enthusiasm for the writing process, too!

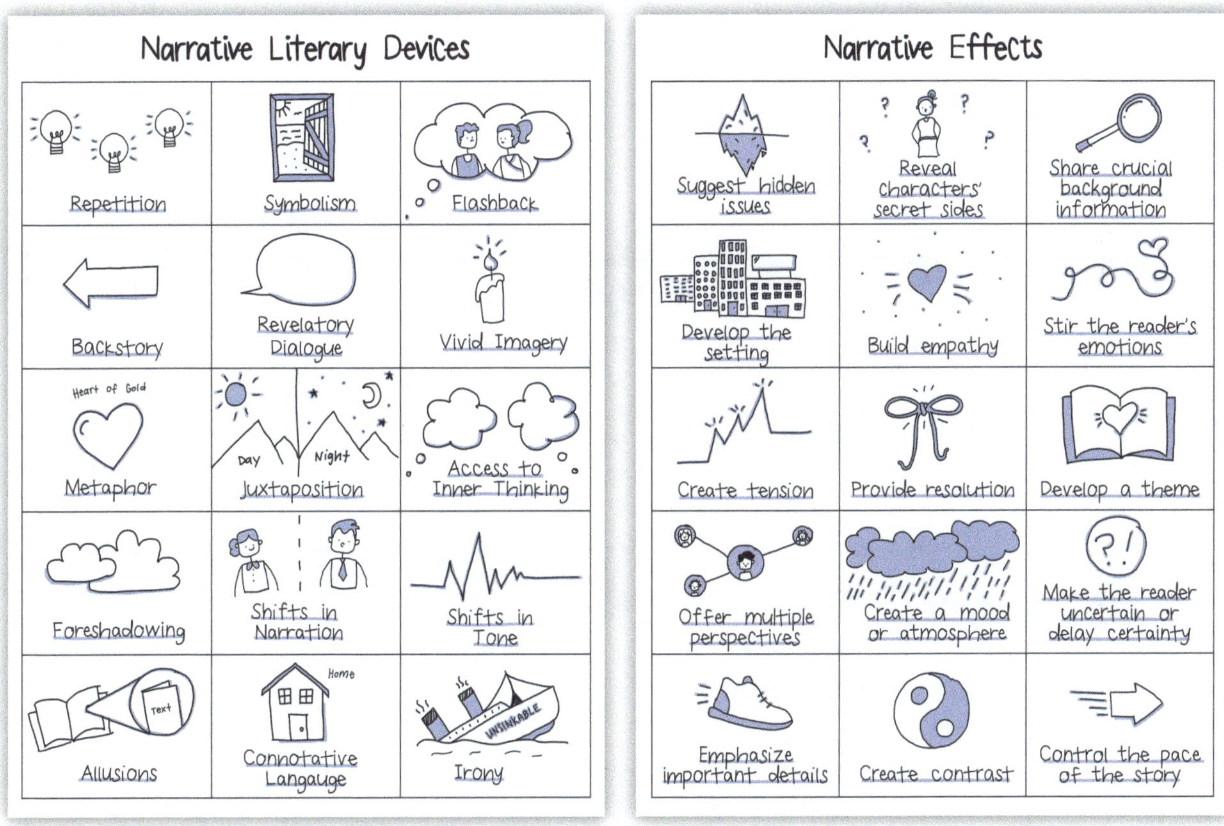

Visual checklists to support revision work. These are introduced in Lesson 1.

Lesson 1

Mentor Text Inquiry (with Visual Checklists)

STRATEGY

Writers often turn to mentor texts to build a repertoire of possible strategies for craft and elaboration. Sometimes they study the mentor texts with a checklist of literary techniques, investigating how writers use these techniques. Other times, writers can create a checklist from a mentor text, by finding and naming moves a writer makes that they admire.

Visit hs-guidetoteaching.org to access visual checklists for narrative literary devices and narrative effects and a recommended collection of memoir mentor texts for teens.

USE THIS STRATEGY...so that writers have a handful of techniques they can try, without waiting for you to teach each one. Teaching young writers to use mentor texts across the writing process also sets them up to lean on mentors anytime they are writing, for any task.

Inquiry Questions

- What literary devices do I notice this writer using?
- What effects does the writer achieve by using those techniques?
- What moves does this writer make that I also want to try?

LAUNCH THE INQUIRY

- Suggest that as writers consider craft and elaboration, they often return to mentor texts to investigate what moves other writers make that they also want to try. Introduce (or remind students of) a selection of mentor texts.
- Invite students to join you in investigating some of the literary devices they notice in one mentor text. We suggest Misa Sugiura's, "Where I'm From" from *Come on In* (Alsaid 2020) because it has very visible craft, and it's available online, but you can lead this inquiry with any favorite memoir. You only need to demonstrate with the first page or so.
- Give students the narrative literary techniques and effects visual checklists as a support.

- Set up students to investigate other favorite mentors. Suggest that they can use the visual chart to help them locate literary devices, or they can also create their own list of craft moves from a text.
- Depending on time, end with students setting goals for what writing moves they want to try in their own piece and beginning the work of going back into their drafts to try some of these moves.

PROMPTS TO COACH STUDENTS AND PARTNERSHIPS

One way to try this work is to think about it as playing a kind of literary bingo, asking yourself: Where do I see these devices in this text, and what effects do I notice?

Some writers tend to use a couple of devices again and again. You can do that too. You can really lean into repetition, or symbolism, for instance, like Misa Sugiura does.

It's also interesting to create your own technique checklist from a mentor text. Grab some sticky notes or create a chart, and begin to fill in what you notice a writer doing. You can also ask an AI partner to help you name some of these techniques.

CLASSROOM ARTIFACTS

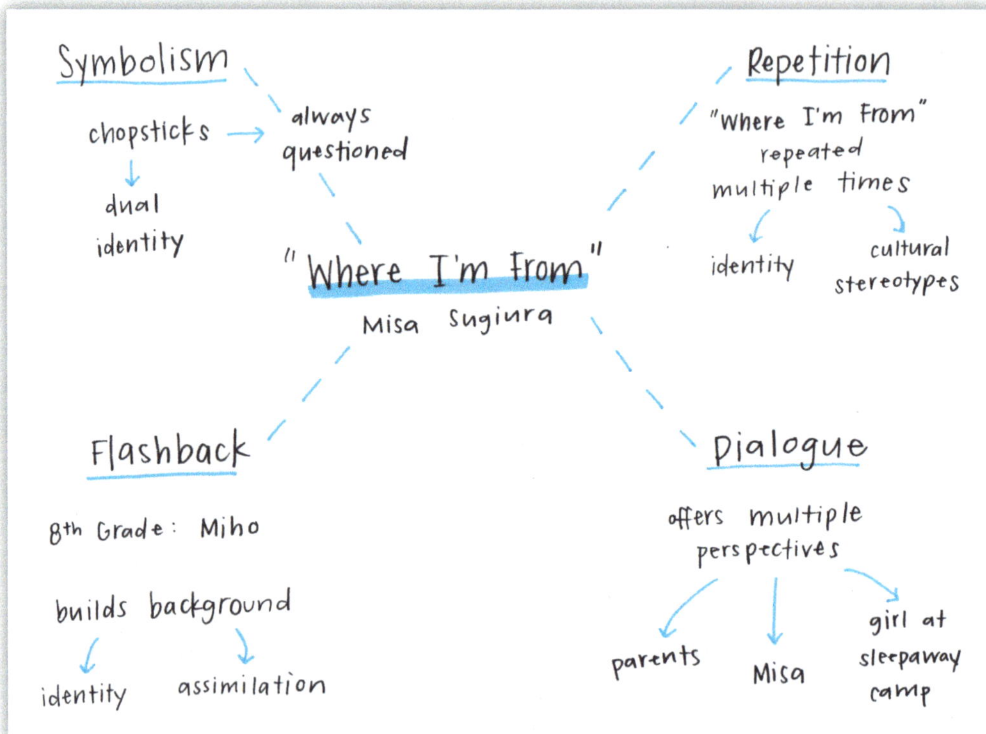

Investigating craft moves in "Where I'm From," by Misa Sugiura.

Honing Dialogue to Reveal Traits and Emotions

Lesson 2

STRATEGY

Narrative writers know that dialogue can accomplish many jobs inside a story, including revealing character traits and emotions and adding tension. Writers, then, don't struggle to remember *exactly* what was said. Instead, they think like a writer, asking what characters *might* say that will capture the truth of how a moment felt.

USE THIS STRATEGY...both for writers who have nothing but dialogue (sometimes common to young writers) and, therefore, are poised to make their dialogue do better work inside their story, and for writers whose narratives are mostly internal, to bring alive other characters and perspectives. Note: There is a lesson on punctuating dialogue in Chapter 4, Lesson 2.

Visit hs-guidetoteaching.org to download a "before and after" demonstration text for this lesson and a teaching chart for developing dialogue.

TEACH THE STRATEGY

- Explain to students that writers don't, usually, tend to remember what precisely was said in any given moment, and so this is an opportunity to use recreated dialogue. It's a way for memoirists to capture the essence and feeling of a conversation, even if they can't recall the exact words spoken.
- Share a chart to support students in thinking about the work dialogue can do in a story.

Narrative writers use dialogue to...	Narrative writers develop their dialogue by...
1. Reveal character traits that are important in the story	1. Reviewing their dialogue to see where it could be more powerful
2. Suggest strong emotions or turmoil	2. Asking: "What might characters say?"
3. Add tension	3. Considering the ways people speak, their language patterns (y'all...)
4. Suggest hidden issues	4. Adding tone of voice and body language

Lesson 2 (Continued)

- Invite students to join you in revising dialogue in a snippet of your memoir to demonstrate how effective this kind of revision can be in making dialogue more powerful. Share an excerpt that you have structured in a way that is ready for dialogue insertion.
- After adding some dialogue with students, review with them the steps you followed, pointing back to your chart. Invite them to look over their draft, and consider where they might do similar work to add dialogue or make their dialogue more powerful.

<u>Just Before the Race</u>

Lisa and I were stretching by the starting line, talking about the race. It was Nationals. The ¼ mile hurdles. A national title. A college scholarship.

Just then Chris came by. Chris, whom I adored. Chris, the fastest boy in New York State. He told me he hoped I'd win.

Chris smiled at Lisa. When he went up into the stands, Lisa turned, and said I wasn't going to win.

Suddenly we saw Mr. Worth, Lisa's dad. Lisa's mom had died two months before, from breast cancer. Since her mom died, Lisa lived alone with her dad, and she was different. She came to school sometimes with bruises on her arms, that she wouldn't talk about. Mr. Worth walked towards us, in a dark T-shirt and jeans, the muscles in his arms bulging. Then he stood, right in front of Lisa, close.

"Listen, Lisa, you better win," he said. His voice was hard and low. "Second place is for losers. And there's no room in this family for losers." He clenched his fist. Lisa paled.

The warning gun for the start went off.

Demonstration writing before revision.

<u>Just Before the Race</u>

Lisa and I were stretching by the starting line, ~~talking about the race~~. It was Nationals. The ¼ mile hurdles. A national title. A college scholarship.

"I wish we could both win," I murmured, sneaking a look at the bruises on Lisa's arm.

"Impossible," Lisa sneered, her eyes turning hard. "And I'm not holding back."

Just then Chris came by. Chris, whom I adored. Chris, the fastest boy in New York State. ~~He told me he hoped I'd win~~. "I hope you win," he whispered, putting his hand on my neck, under my hair, the way I loved. "I love how fast you are."

Chris smiled at Lisa. When he went up into the stands, Lisa turned, ~~and said I wasn't going to win~~. She whispered, fiercely, "You're not going to win, you know. Not the race, and not with Chris, either."

Suddenly we saw Mr. Worth, Lisa's dad. Lisa's mom had died two months before, from breast cancer. Since her mom died, Lisa lived alone with her dad, and she was different. She came to school sometimes with bruises on her arms, that she wouldn't talk about. Mr. Worth walked towards us, in a dark T-shirt and jeans, the muscles in his arms bulging. Then he stood, right in front of Lisa, close.

Demonstration writing after revision, with dialogue added.

When Mary invited students to join her in thinking about how to add dialogue to her piece, she set up her initial excerpt so that it had cues for dialogue insertion (talking about the race. . . he told me. . . she said. . .). She also inserted white space, to open up the piece to revision. Finally, Mary made sure there wasn't a lot of other distracting craft, such as setting details, so her text could be short and students could focus on dialogue. Often, it's easier to draft a small excerpt, so that it is set up well for what you are going to teach.

PROMPTS TO COACH STUDENTS AND PARTNERSHIPS

Sometimes you realize that you already have a lot of dialogue, and then the question you can ask yourself is: Which lines of dialogue are most powerful and why? Where does my story need dialogue?

If you don't have any dialogue in your story, ask yourself if dialogue might help develop the perspective of other characters.

Adding tone of voice and body language has a surprising effect. It often adds to tension in a story. You can think about how it can either contrast or reinforce what is said.

CLASSROOM ARTIFACTS

> I was sitting in the nail salon just minding my own business when a stranger felt the urge to strike up a conversation, a conversation about my Vitiligo. I try to always be polite when I find myself in these uncomfortable situations, as if I need to accommodate the intrusive person, but when she began with asking me if I get made fun of in school for the way I look, all I was only able to get out was one word: No.

A writer's first draft before experimenting with dialogue.

> I was sitting in the nail salon just minding my own business when a stranger felt the urge to strike up a conversation, a conversation about my Vitiligo.
>
> **"Do you get made fun of in school for the way you look?"**
>
> I try to always be polite when I find myself in these uncomfortable situations, as if I need to accommodate the intrusive person, but all I was able to get out was one word, *quiet, and quick.*
>
> **"No."**

The writer added dialogue that introduces tension.

Lesson 3

Slowing Down the Tension

STRATEGY

Often, when drafting personal stories, writers rush through the tension, perhaps because it is painful or because it happened quickly. But readers want to linger in the conflict. Writers, then, can study mentors for techniques to slow down these moments, and they can make the trouble a major part of their revision and elaboration.

Visit hs-guidetoteaching.org to download a sample demonstration text for this inquiry and a teaching chart.

USE THIS STRATEGY... to help your writers study literary techniques, learn from mentor texts, and elaborate their own moments of greatest tension in their memoirs.

Inquiry Questions

- How do writers slow down and develop tension?
- What moves can I learn from other writers that I might like to try in my own writing?

LAUNCH THE INQUIRY

- Suggest to students that when drafting their own, true stories, writers often move quickly through the moments of greatest tension, which are of great interest to the reader. It's worth it, then, in revision, to return to these moments of tension or trouble and develop them.
- Introduce a mentor demonstration text (we use part of Mary's memoir) that employs multiple, visible techniques, and invite students to study the text, asking the first inquiry question: How does this writer slow down or develop the moment of trouble?
- As students name the parts of the text they notice and the techniques involved, you can generate a chart of these literary techniques to support your writers.
    - Some students don't have the literary language for these techniques quite yet, and they tend to talk about the parts they like. Then you can summarize what they say and name the literary technique.

- For students who need extra support, you could jot techniques on sticky notes first and invite them to find places where the demonstration text uses that technique.

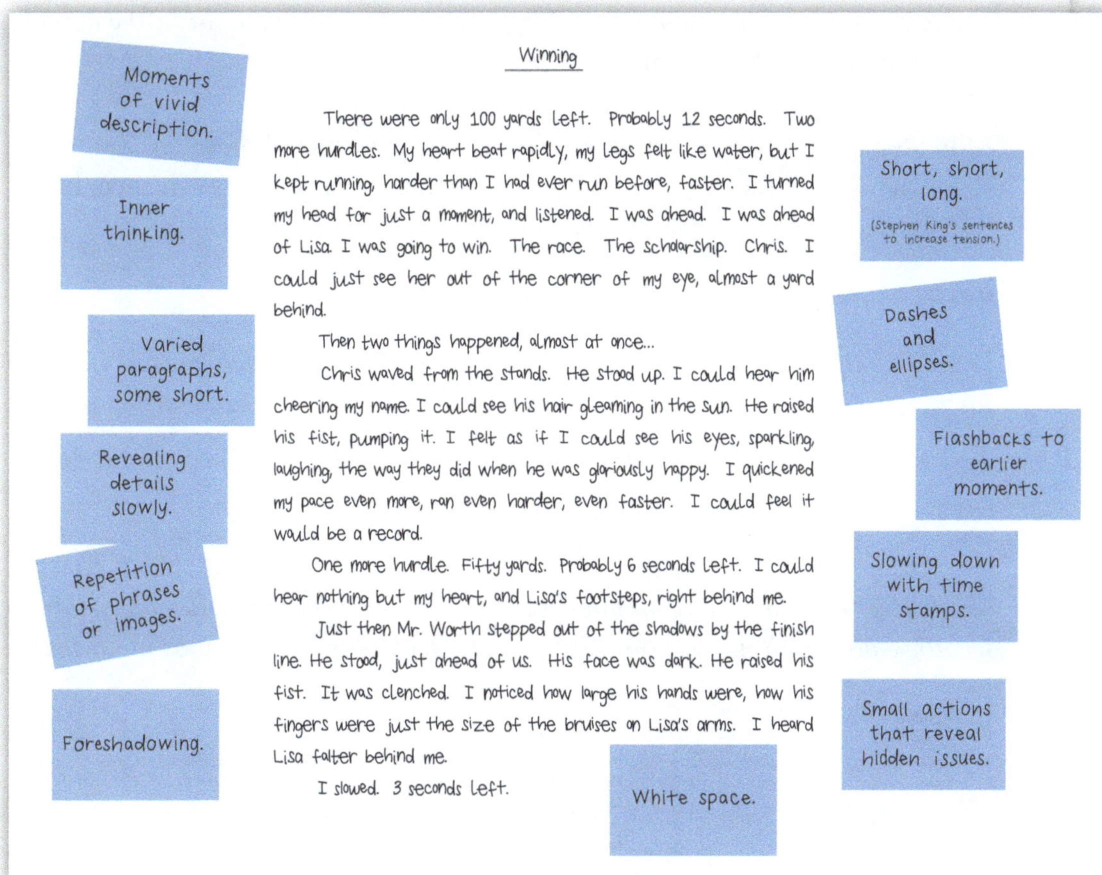

Winning

There were only 100 yards left. Probably 12 seconds. Two more hurdles. My heart beat rapidly, my legs felt like water, but I kept running, harder than I had ever run before, faster. I turned my head for just a moment, and listened. I was ahead. I was ahead of Lisa. I was going to win. The race. The scholarship. Chris. I could just see her out of the corner of my eye, almost a yard behind.

Then two things happened, almost at once...

Chris waved from the stands. He stood up. I could hear him cheering my name. I could see his hair gleaming in the sun. He raised his fist, pumping it. I felt as if I could see his eyes, sparkling, laughing, the way they did when he was gloriously happy. I quickened my pace even more, ran even harder, even faster. I could feel it would be a record.

One more hurdle. Fifty yards. Probably 6 seconds left. I could hear nothing but my heart, and Lisa's footsteps, right behind me.

Just then Mr. Worth stepped out of the shadows by the finish line. He stood, just ahead of us. His face was dark. He raised his fist. It was clenched. I noticed how large his hands were, how his fingers were just the size of the bruises on Lisa's arms. I heard Lisa falter behind me.

I slowed. 3 seconds left.

When Mary did this work with a class, she wrote a demonstration text that combined a lot of the techniques that writers use in one short excerpt, so her students could easily see several visible techniques. She first annotated the text and captured the techniques on sticky notes, and then moved the sticky notes over to a chart that students can use.

- Invite students to tell their partner which of these techniques they want to try, have them identify the moment(s) of greatest tension in their memoirs, and send them off to elaborate.

PROMPTS TO COACH STUDENTS AND PARTNERSHIPS

It can be helpful to try out a couple of techniques and see which ones work best for your memoir. You can use the list we generated as a class as a starting point.

This is a great time to lean on your writing partner, or even your AI partner, to ask about which moments are the best to stretch out.

Your memoir might be one that doesn't have a clear conflict or problem. That's okay. This is about finding an important moment and slowing it down, so we feel the emotion alongside you. Which parts feel highly emotional or important?

CLASSROOM ARTIFACTS

> I just wanted to blend in. If I could've blended into the walls like some sort of chameleon, I would have. I didn't feel like myself throughout middle school and my clothing reflected that. No bright colors, no dresses, no jewelry or accessories. I even renounced my favorite color (pink). I changed, but it wasn't for the better; I was suffocating myself.

The first draft before stretching out the moment.

> I just wanted to blend in. If I could've blended into the walls like some sort of chameleon, I would have. I didn't feel like myself throughout middle school and my clothing reflected that.
>
> **I looked in my closet and saw the brightly colored tops and fun patterned dresses. I ran my fingertips over the silky fabrics, wishing I could just wear what I love. Instead, I flipped through the hangers until I got to the black band t-shirts. Without much thought I slipped one over my head and then turned to face the full length mirror.** No bright colors, no dresses, no jewelry, no accessories. **I let out an audible sigh. *This is as good as it's going to get.***
>
> **When would I realize I was suffocating myself?**

In the revision, the narrative writer slows down a moment of tension with inner thinking.

Weaving Reflection Throughout Memoir

Lesson 4

STRATEGY

Memoir writers develop the reflective parts of their narratives, which often serve as a way to think back on moments, issues, or relationships in our lives. Sometimes responding to thought prompts with a partner helps a writer come to new realizations and insights.

USE THIS STRATEGY...to support writers in framing their narrative moments with reflection. Thought prompts can also help students think about what their story is really about.

Visit hs-guidetoteaching.org to access thought prompt cards.

TEACH THE STRATEGY

- Suggest to students that memoir writers not only develop the narrative parts of their stories, they also weave in reflection to highlight how they've grown since the time of their story, either in terms of new realizations or through other changes.
- Introduce the collection of thought prompt cards, and demonstrate inviting a partner to prompt you about your own story.

Thought Prompt Cards for Memoir

When I think about this now...	Later I realized...	I was never really able to figure out...
I still wonder...	Others would never know that...	What I was too young to understand then...
I think this story is really about...	What still feels complicated about this moment is...	Writing about this has helped me figure out...

Lesson 4 (Continued)

- After talking aloud with your partner, model making a few revisions to your writing, showing how the memoir deepens when you add reflection.
- End by setting up students in partnerships to develop the reflective parts of their essay, using these thought prompts.

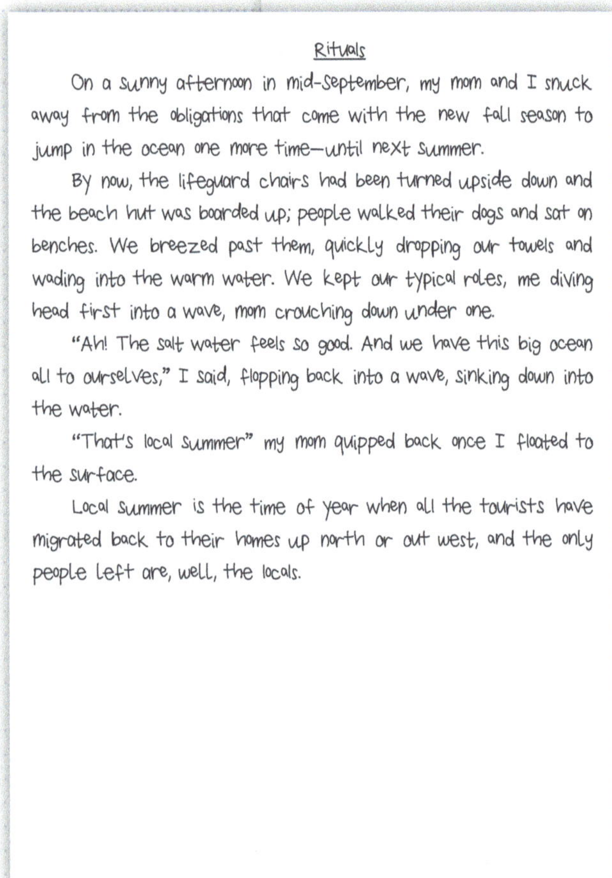

Demonstration writing before revision.

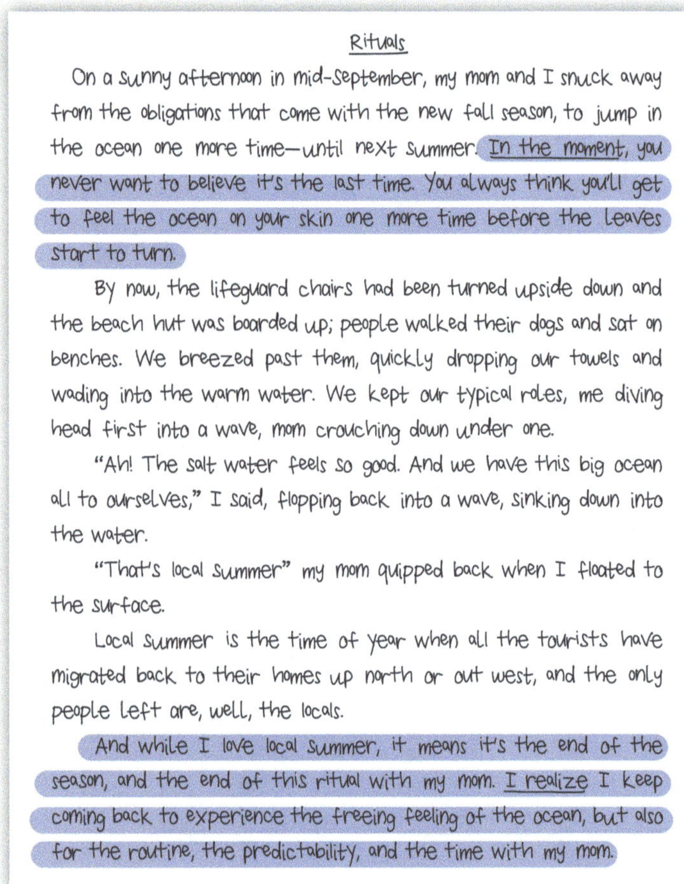

Demonstration writing after revision.

Coley demonstrated adding in a few moments of reflection to two different parts of her draft, deciding in front of students which scenes would benefit from reflection.

If you do the same, invite a student or two to play the role of your partner, leading you with a card they choose. You may be surprised at the new content you discover!

PROMPTS TO COACH STUDENTS AND PARTNERSHIPS

Often it helps to simply talk through these thought prompts. But you might record yourself, so you can watch the video after, to see what parts of your thinking you want to add to your memoir.

What you're really doing is explaining why this moment has stayed with you, why it feels important. Sometimes you can simply open your notebook and jot an explanation and then add that to your memoir.

It helps sometimes, to look at other writers who have extensively developed the reflective parts of their memoirs. Renée Watson, in "Black Like Me," for instance, beautifully balances story, reflection, and argument.

CLASSROOM ARTIFACTS

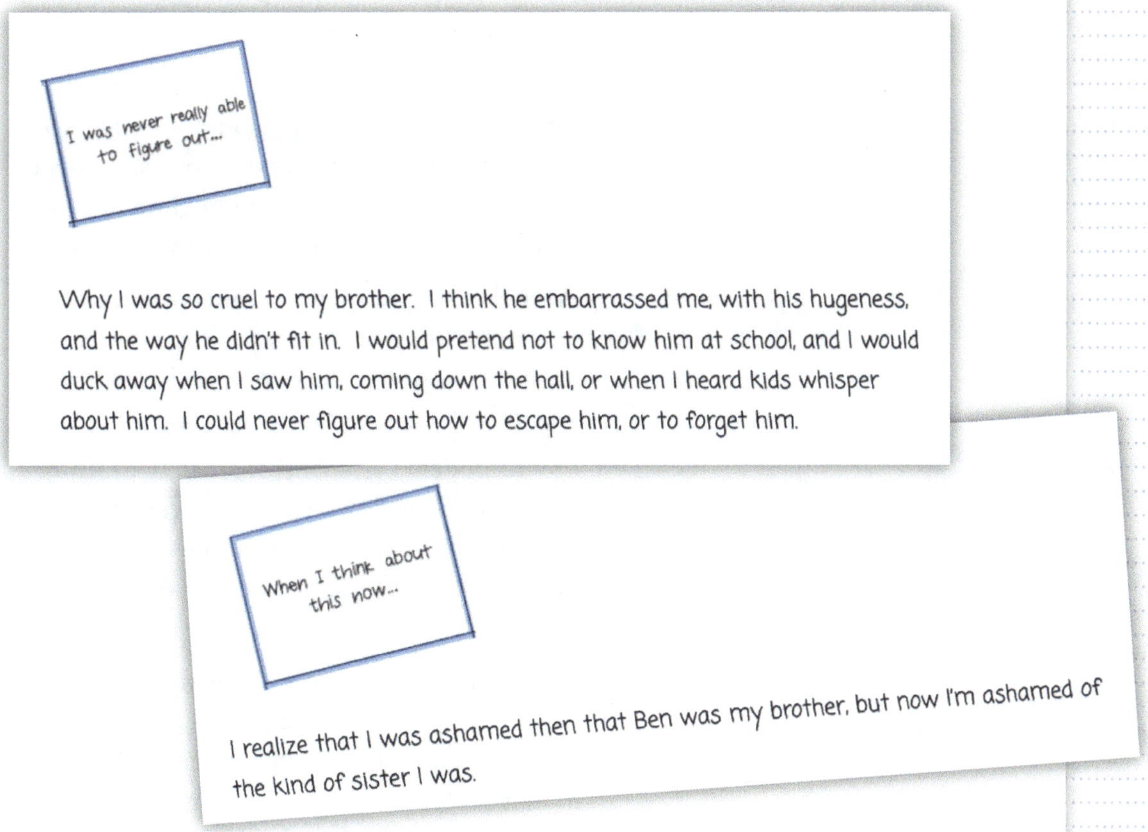

Using prompts to guide reflection.

Lesson 5

Using Poetry to Mine Figurative Language and Imagery

STRATEGY

Writers often turn to poetry to find figurative and poetic language to use in their memoirs. Writers can also rewrite a snippet of their memoir as a poem or imagine how their entire memoir would sound as a narrative poem.

Visit hs-guidetoteaching.org for a collection of beautiful poems to use as mentor texts.

USE THIS STRATEGY...to help your writers craft vivid imagery, develop evocative language, and overall achieve a more unleashed quality to their memoir. Poetry often sparks inspiration in a writer, no matter the genre they write within.

TEACH THE STRATEGY

- Suggest to students that no matter what genre they are writing, writers often turn to poetry to find figurative and poetic language.

Chris

When he was twelve
Chris was the most beautiful boy ever seen
in our neighborhood...
in our school...
maybe in the universe
His gilded beauty was something glimmering, glorious, galactic
By the time he was sixteen
Your heart would falter when Chris approached
Boy or girl, man or woman, it didn't matter
Your heart would falter.
Even dogs would lay down and roll over
Exposing not only their bellies but their hearts
Hoping for the softness of Chris's gossamer touch and the
susurration of his whispered, "aren't you lovely, darling."

- Demonstrate, for instance, how you might imagine the start of a poem about one part of your memoir. Then invite your students to consider with you how you might add some language, or the poem itself, to your piece.
- Model how you might consider adding phrases from your poem back into your memoir, as well as how you could insert the poem into your memoir.
- Invite students to spend some time drafting "the poem they'd start, if they were to write a poem." If students need some inspiration, they might read or watch some mentor poems.
- End by having partners share and talk about where and how they might insert poetry into their memoir. Suggest that some students might prefer poetry for their entire memoir.

When Mary did this with her class, she returned to a part of her memoir that her students would know by now, about a boy she loved in high school, and imagined how a poem might start. It often helps to say to students, "How might you start, if you were to write a poem?"

PROMPTS TO COACH STUDENTS AND PARTNERSHIPS

Don't fret about writing good poetry. Just say, "How might a poem about this start?" and go for it!

Sometimes a good place to start is to try "I am" poems or "Where I'm from" poems, which lead almost immediately into writing about your identity.

It can help, sometimes, to listen to young poets tell their stories, and hear how evocative their language is. You might watch Emi Mahmoud, for example, or Elizabeth Acevedo and use some of their language and literary devices as inspiration for your memoir.

CLASSROOM ARTIFACTS

Underwater

Silence fills the space, surrounded by solid **DARK**.
No vision, but life floats around you.
Lungs crave life, but your mind craves peace.
Here you can decide what is most important.

Slowly sinking, in the depths the ground is **COLD**.
Not knowing what lies beyond.
You pass your comfort zone.
Further away from your own understanding.

Ascending up, you start to open your eyes to **LIGHT**.
Your ears restore, listening to the soft crash of life.
Walking back once again to familiar surroundings.

It was the middle of August, waves were 8–10 feet, biggest swells of the season. My shift just ended, and low tide was finally going out. I grab my surfboard from my car, put on my leash and hop into the now dirty water caused by the impact of the waves. It was a red flag day meaning nobody besides lifeguards were allowed in the water. Paddling my board out into water waves come crashing down, barely making it out without drowning a bit. I see the first set coming in. I pivot on my board, but I bail out because I was way too scared to catch waves of this caliber for the first time. I splash water on my face and get ready for the next wave, I begin to paddle but drop in too late and completely tumble, gripping onto my board under the icy water. **Silence fills the space.** I struggle to breath. I manage to scramble my way onto the board before the next set comes in, I begin my way back out into the water.

As I sit out in the dark water, drifting over massive waves I build up the courage to go for another wave, I see another large set stirring up on the horizon. I begin to set myself up on the board, I hear people on the pier above me yelling and pointing at this huge wave incoming. The tail of my board begins to go upward, once I reach the lip I drop in, flying down the face of the wave with such speed. The barrel begins to incase me, faster than anything on earth. Then the nose of the board hits the side of the face. Flipping my board into a spiral I fall and get hammered down by this wave.

I feel my body getting tossed by the might and power of the ocean. ***Slowly sinking, in the depths the ground is cold.*** Struggling to bring my body up to the surface I feel the weight from my leg where my leash was attached become very light. Looking down at my foot I see half a board. Frantically looking around in the water for the other half I run out of the water, the top half of my board washes up on the sand in two. Sitting there defeated knees in the sand, ***I can hear in the back the soft crash of life,*** then my coworkers laughing at me comes back into focus.

This writer culled language from his poetry to add poetic language to his narrative.

Lesson 6

Coaching Your AI Partner to Personalize Its Feedback

Visit hs-guidetoteaching.org to access a chart on tips for coaching AI to personalize its feedback.

STRATEGY

Professional writers know that AI can be a helpful feedback partner, especially once they've written a draft. To personalize the feedback they'll get, and to use that feedback to make them stronger, writers give their AI partner a lot of information, and sometimes tools, that will shape that feedback.

USE THIS STRATEGY...to help your students learn how to use AI wisely, as a partner in the writing process, not a replacement writer. This strategy will also coach your students in personalizing their interactions with AI. If you can, set students up with EdTech AI such as Flint or MagicSchool.

TEACH THE STRATEGY

- Suggest to students that writers often turn to AI to get feedback on their drafts, and they experiment with prompting their AI partner to get the most personal, helpful feedback possible.
    - Set up students with EdTech AI if possible, and set the parameters so it won't draft for students.
    - If setting up students with OpenAI, coach them to train their AI partner carefully.
- Share a chart of ways to coach your AI partner.

Coach your AI Partner for Better Feedback

1. Define Your Goals	2. Share Your Journey	3. Provide Helpful Context
· My goals for my writing are...	· As a writer, in the past I've...	· I've uploaded earlier pieces, so you can comment on growth or patterns.
· I think my piece is really about...	· I'm finding it difficult to...	· I've uploaded a mentor, so you know what I'm striving for.
· I want help first with one thing/part, and I want you to make multiple suggestions.	· I'm proud of...	· I've uploaded a rubric or checklist so you knows how I'll be assessed.
· Please share three specific examples of how I might try...		

- Model how you might prompt your AI partner, as shown in the Classroom Artifacts.
- Invite students to do similar work, practicing prompting their AI partner to support their work with feedback suggestions. Insist that students have a draft before beginning this work!

PROMPTS TO COACH STUDENTS AND PARTNERSHIPS

Talk to your AI partner like it's an intelligent writer who wants to help. Tell it what you'd most like help with. But don't let your AI partner take over. Make sure it's helping you grow, not taking your place. For example, if it provides sample writing, make sure to rewrite that in your own words, if you take one of those suggestions.

You might want to upload just one part of your draft at a time. Sometimes AI is helpful when it knows the whole story, but it can also give more specific feedback when you just share one section. You can decide what works best for you.

Always ask for multiple suggestions. Then you can consider and make choices. You can also ask your AI partner to explain its suggestions, so you can get some tips as a writer.

CLASSROOM ARTIFACTS

> I am writing a memoir about when my youngest brother had his first seizure. I think it's really about the roles we took on in my family—how we react when things are difficult, and how we express the love we feel for each other. I'm finding it difficult to really bring out and show the role I play, because I feel like I'm stuck in the medical details. I want to show not just what happened with my brother, but how I reacted—how I really stepped up as a big sister, and how I worked to take care of my other younger brother, and my parents. I've uploaded my draft. I'm not uploading the rubric yet because I want your feedback first on the part where my brother is in the hospital, and we are all still waiting for news.

Lauren drafts a prompt in front of her students, emphasizing helpful sentence starters, such as "I'm writing about …" and "I'm finding it difficult to …"

Lesson 7

Making Linguistic Choices

STRATEGY

Writers know that it can be hard to develop confidence in your own voice, and they help each other develop this confidence. It can help to study writers who have worked hard to articulate their own linguistic consciousness, such as Jamila Lyiscott.

Access Jamila Lyiscott's TED Talk, "3 Ways to Speak English," on YouTube.

USE THIS STRATEGY...to help students explore register, voice, and idiom to develop their own voice and give voice to established characters in their memoir.

TEACH THE STRATEGY

- Suggest to students that memoir is an opportunity for writers to develop their own voices, to make what we call linguistic choices, or choices about language, tone, idiom, and word choice. For instance, they might use more than one language, like Elizabeth Acevedo and Junot Diaz often do, or they might speak colloquially—how they speak with friends, the way Jason Reynolds often does in his writing.
- Invite students to watch Jamila Lyiscott's TED Talk, "3 Ways to Speak English," and to share with each other what they admire about what she talks about and how she manipulates/liberates language in this talk.
- Create a chart of the moves Jamila Lyiscott makes in this talk.
- Suggest writers talk to their partner about how they tend to write and speak at school, with their friends, and in other spaces, and to apply any implications for their linguistic choices in all or part of their memoir.

What Jamila Lyiscott Does in Her TED Talk

- slips into and out of poetry
- emphasizes repetition + rhyme scheme
- speaks in characters' voices + languages
- shifts the way she talks in different situations
- asks questions about representation
- questions authority
- celebrates linguistic histories
- articulates different forms of English
- makes arguments about power + language
- shares emotional ties to language
- reconceptualizes TED Talk modality

PROMPTS TO COACH STUDENTS AND PARTNERSHIPS

There might be ways you speak outside of school that you want to articulate in this memoir.

Sometimes you can think about particular characters—friends and family members—and how they speak.

Language choices reflect power, and your language choices can assert power. How do you want to speak in this piece?

CLASSROOM ARTIFACTS

Lo que no te mata, engorda" or literally, that which doesn't kill you makes you fatter, is something that has been said often in my family. But I think the intent of the saying is that it makes you stronger. My family certainly takes this advice seriously. Thin is frail and fragile. Fat is robust and healthy. Food is a part of our family life and part of every family event.

My nomadic lifestyle is core to who I am. I've gotten comfortable being myself and trusting that, when encountered with a new environment, I'll be able to jump into the abyss and figure it out. The process is excruciating, but the transitory emotional toll pays over tenfold in character, experience and knowledge. I'd describe myself now as:

> Resilient-flexible-adaptive-extroverted-amicable-sensitive-open-diverse-curious-engaged -culturally-aware-thoughtful-friendly-relaxed-dignified-competitive-ambitious-intellectu al-knowledgeable-cultured-tolerant

These writers experiment with language in their narratives.

Lesson 8

Layering Expository Writing Within Memoir

Visit hs-guidetoteaching.org to access an annotated mentor text.

STRATEGY

Memoirists sometimes include outside information and expository writing in their memoirs. They do this by thinking about what information would be beneficial and engaging to the reader, conducting research, and then trying out a few places where the information might fit. Sometimes memoir writers suggest a claim or argument, and research helps them support it.

USE THIS STRATEGY... when writers have memoirs that would benefit from research or outside information, or the writer is suggesting a claim about a topic in their memoir.

TEACH THE STRATEGY

- Suggest to students that memoirs sometimes have parts other than narrative, and that these expository parts often add layers of information that make the memoir more complex.
- Invite students to study a memoir that has a few expository parts with you, asking them to notice the expository elements the writer has included and why. We recommend "Googling Strangers" or "Scratch 'n' Sniff Stickers" from John Green's book *The Anthropocene Reviewed* (2021). Annotate the memoir as part of your demonstration.

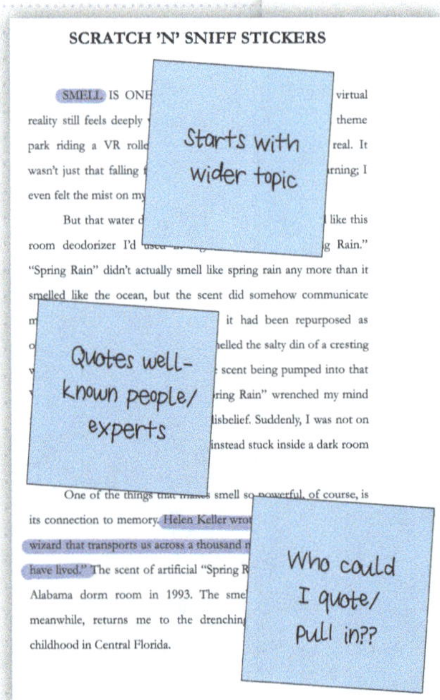

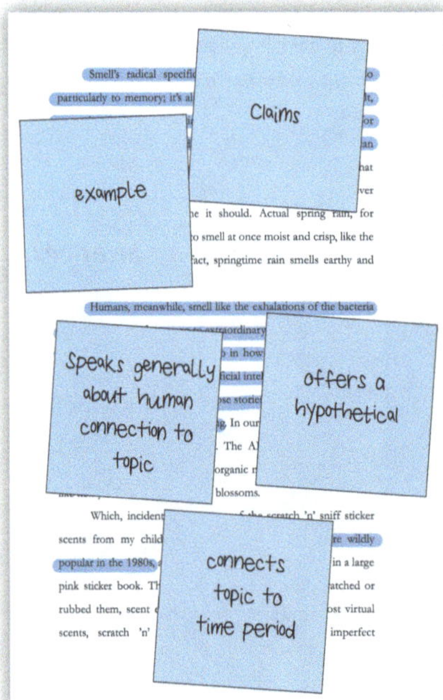

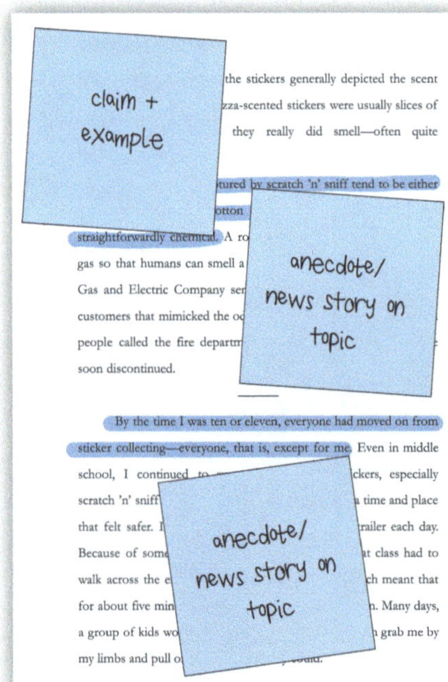

- Model the process of adding in expository writing into your own memoir.

> Ocean Grove
>
> For my mom and me, Ocean Grove is more than just a beach– it's memories and rituals and love. This town has watched me grow up. It saw me when I got my braces off and when I hobbled onto the beach with a full leg cast. And it heard me as I talked and talked about my dreams for the future.
>
> Of course, this isn't just true for me. Ocean Grove, founded in 1869, serves as a place of sentimentality for so many people. Walking through the town you see Nagles Soda Fountain, and big Victorian houses with wrap-around porches, and even a tent community that dates back to 1870s. It's like stepping back in time both in the landscape and in my own life.
>
> It's the start of a new season, so it's time to pick up our beach badges. We take the winding walk to the booth eager for a new season with the same routines.

When Coley demonstrated, she first did a think-aloud about which parts of her memoir could come more alive by adding information. She decided to explore Ocean Grove specifically. Coley briefly showed the research she did—finding websites, a video, and an image—and then she returned to her draft to weave in these expository details.

- Invite students to talk to their partner about whether, and how, they might like to try this strategy to add to their own memoir, and send them off to work, letting them know you're available for support with research.

PROMPTS TO COACH STUDENTS AND PARTNERSHIPS

It can be helpful to lean on mentor texts to see how they integrate expository writing into their memoirs. Look at a few of these and see what you're noticing.

You'll want to cite your sources and embed quotes or paraphrase, similar to how you would in an essay.

You could try adding in some expository writing in one specific part, or weaving it throughout. Maybe try it both ways and see what works best for your memoir.

CLASSROOM ARTIFACTS

When you're in the womb as an embryo, your head and trunk are the first biological structures to develop. Microscopic limb buds form, which will later flourish and develop into your arms and legs. Next is your brain. Cranial nerves begin coursing all throughout your head, taking control of your senses. Then your face, then your heart. Blood begins to pulse, exploring chambers, capillaries, and vessels. At about ½ inch, almost all of your facial features will have developed. The upper lip, the nose, and the ears. At this point, your cells have already decided what you will look like as you grow up.

Those tiny microscopic cells which determine our physical traits are so much smaller than the overwhelming problem of insecurity. Every person on this planet has experienced it to varying degrees. I've even battled with it myself, even though I am generally a pretty confident person. People have commented on my posture when I walk, my nose shape, my forehead, and my body - all things that I wasn't insecure about previously. At times I've been so focused on trying to fix or hide something about myself for others, that I've forgotten what it feels like to be happy with who I am.

This young writer weaves biology into her memoir about insecurity and fitting in.

You, and the Stranger

Lesson 9

STRATEGY

Stephen King (2010, 2021) speaks about how writers have to keep in mind two audiences: themselves and the stranger. Memoirists attend to "the stranger" by considering all the background information, setting details, and other details that their reader might not know.

USE THIS STRATEGY...to help writers attend to detail and to write with a sense of audience in mind.

TEACH THE STRATEGY

- You might quote Stephen King, who in his novel *Billy Summers* (2021) speaks of how writers have to keep two audiences in mind: themselves and a stranger. For the stranger, they have to explain the small details that the narrator already knows.
- Share a snippet of a memoir—a few lean lines that leave students with lots of questions—and invite students to share with a partner what details it leaves them wondering about.
- Demonstrate how you might add one or two of these details, so "the stranger" would better understand your scene.

We stretched in front of the starting line, thinking about who would win. At least, that's what I was thinking about. I'm sure Lisa was too.

We stretched in front of the starting line, thinking about who would win. It was Nationals. The ¼ mile hurdles. A national title. A college scholarship. At least, that's what I was thinking about. I'm sure Lisa was too. Lisa, who had been my best friend since kindergarten, who ran away with me when we were seven, and then stapled her finger to mine, to show our loyalty.

When Mary invited students to think about this small snippet from her memoir, students had many questions—what race, what kind of race, who was Lisa, who was faster, how did they both end up in this race. After listening to the students' questions, Mary drafted a few new lines, tucking in background information on the race and Lisa.

- Invite students trade their memoirs with their partner, and suggest that partners play the role of "the stranger," marking places where they have questions about details. Then suggest writers get to work adding some of those details.

PROMPTS TO COACH STUDENTS AND PARTNERSHIPS

It can be helpful to imagine you're writing fiction sometimes, because then you'd expect to have to share all the details the reader would need.

Some writers close their eyes and picture the scene like a movie scene and then fill in all those details, especially of the setting.

Sometimes this work involves sharing a back story, and you can do that through inner thinking or a flashback.

CLASSROOM ARTIFACTS

The backcountry snow of the Colorado Rockies stretches out for fathoms around me. There is something about the empty silence that makes me want to break it, even in the most mundane way, by reaching for a phone that can only connect me to people a thousand miles away, in a different place entirely.

I settle in, lean back on my heels, and think back to the day we were here last, a year ago. **He and I. Collin, ski patrol guide, my mentor here in these woods.** Collin is showing me the ice pit he wants me to crawl into. **We are training the avalanche dogs to find bodies.** The pit is narrow and dark.

I look at the pit, then at Collin. **I see his worn leather gloves, his red patrol jacket that has faded from the high-altitude sunlight, the battered radio, the pulsing avalanche beacon.** His steady gaze. I climb in, headfirst. Inside, it is dark and cold and I sense the weight of the mountain pushing down on me. Collin closes the pit. **First, he puts chunks of ice over the opening. Then he puts snow, then he puts a scree of rocks. I hear a groaning sound. It's the ice and snow moving around me.** I can't hear Collin, but I know he's climbing up, to release the dog from the top of the mountain. It's black inside the hole. Then I hear the music. **It is a music that emerges from the noise of the ice.** A symphony that right now, in the whole world, only I can hear. I like thinking about who else has heard this music before me. I think that I'll have to ask Collin about the music. Did he hear it, when he lay in these ice pits?

This writer adds new, specific details to bring his scene alive for "the stranger."

Chapter Four: Experimenting with Artful Conventions

When we think about artful conventions, especially related to narrative writing, we think especially about paragraphing and white space, about sentence structure, about verbs, and about punctuation.

Let's move backward through that list and think first about punctuation. In Lynne Truss's *Eats, Shoots & Leaves: The Zero Tolerance Approach to Punctuation* (2006), she suggests that punctuation shapes meaning. She shares a "Dear Jack" letter and asks readers to repunctuate it, without changing any words or word order to change the meaning (visit hs-guidetoteaching.org to read this text). We love using her work with students, inviting them to repunctuate excerpts to change the meaning.

We've found that when we teach how ending punctuation affects tone, it gets students to pay attention to their ending punctuation again, which is also a good thing, as surprisingly, older students can be forgetful with their ending punctuation, their minds trained by many hours imprinting on social media, which has different codes for conventions.

Punctuating dialogue, on the other hand, involves a lot of tricky, detailed, specific knowledge, depending on what kind of dialogue students write. Rather than trying to convey all of this knowledge through direct instruction, we suggest that you engage students in inquiry, studying what they can learn from how published writers punctuate their dialogue. Meanwhile, this experience also reminds students that they can study published writers for tricky conventions, anytime.

Teaching sentence structure is a lot like teaching how to punctuate dialogue—there are simply so many gorgeous sentence structures, and it's impossible to teach them all. If you love to teach artful grammar, you should have Roy Peter Clark's *Writing Tools: 55 Essential Strategies for Every Writer* (2016). Part I, "Nuts and Bolts," is a short collection of entrancing grammar lessons, including our favorite, "Establish a pattern, then give it a twist." We decided to include one specific lesson on parentheticals (easily expanded to appositives) to lure students into finding sentence structure enticing, followed by an inquiry lesson on mimetic writing, where students mentor themselves to published writers at the sentence level, something Mary, how do you want to write this? Mary Ehrenworth and Vicky Vinton explored in *The Power of Grammar* (2005), and that Jeff Anderson et al. do beautifully, with whole excerpts as well as sentences, in *Patterns of Power, Grades 9–12* (2022).

You'll also find lessons on narrative paragraphs. Roy Peter Clark has a lot to say about paragraphs, especially about ending them powerfully, the power of white space, and the power of the very short paragraph (2016). There is no *rule* about when to paragraph in narrative writing, so this is a good opportunity to remind your writers to think about their readers. Readers appreciate paragraphs for several reasons, from dramatic effect to how they call attention to changes in the text.

Probably the trickiest convention we tackle here, and suggest you tackle as well, is attending to verbs. Verb endings in English are ridiculously complicated, and no student is going to learn 200 irregular verbs through memorization. They'll mostly learn verb endings through reading, which is how so much literary syntax and grammar are absorbed, as incidental learning. But we can first get them to care about verbs as powerful forces in narrative writing. Then we can intrigue them with how verbs suggest time shifts. Then we can suggest that verb endings do matter, and they can use digital tools to help check these verb endings.

Let's say a bit more about digital tools. Narrative writing allows you to explore conventions in artful ways that reinvigorate (or launch) young writers' interest in conventions. We suggest, therefore, teaching lessons and engaging students in inquiry around conventions, so they increase their expertise. That's different from checking your writing for readability and accuracy. There are great digital tools now for writers to "check" their grammar and spelling. Google Docs does a good job, Microsoft Word does a great job, and AI can do an entirely comprehensive (sometimes too comprehensive) edit for meaning as well as conventions. Because your writers will be increasingly turning to AI, we focused on how multilingual learners can benefit from AI translation (and how to train and use these tools wisely), and how all young writers should learn to train an AI partner to know and sustain their voice, style, and content. As always, AI is a powerful tool in helping any writer communicate clearly, but it needs training and harnessing so that it doesn't replace the writer. To learn more about EdTech AI, and training AI as a writing partner, we suggest you turn to *AI-Enhanced Literacy*, by Ehrenworth and Seyfried (2025).

When you're teaching conventions, it's important to teach them as just that—conventions rather than rules. We adhere to the work of Dr. April Baker Bell, author of *Linguistic Justice* (2020), and Jamila Lyiscott, whose "3 Ways to Speak English" (2014) demonstrates the many forms of English that are a powerful force in the world. English is a fluid language, influenced by many sources, ever-changing, and existing in many idioms around the world and in a single neighborhood. Memoir is a place where students' home idioms are easily celebrated.

The lessons in this chapter are all about artful conventions. We'll end here by sharing an editing checklist for students to double-check their writing here, as well—it's a conventional conventions checklist! It's very hard to edit your own writing, but it's also helpful for students to have a quick way to review some of the obvious things, so they are aware of their own patterns as writers.

An Editing Checklist for Narrative Writers

Structure

- ☐ I reviewed my narrative paragraphs, thinking about how they support my readers in noticing:
  - ☐ new characters.
  - ☐ changes in setting.
  - ☐ shifts in time.
- ☐ I considered my paragraph lengths, thinking about the power of occasional short paragraphs for dramatic effect.
- ☐ I reviewed that all paragraphs are properly indented.

Style & Voice

- ☐ I varied my sentence lengths and structures to create rhythm and keep the reader engaged.
- ☐ In places where I'm breaking rules (e.g., deliberate fragments, capitalization, punctuation), I checked that these choices are purposeful.
- ☐ I made linguistic choices (translanguaging, register, idiom).

Dialogue

- ☐ I reviewed my dialogue, looking to a mentor text to double-check punctuation, considering:
  - ☐ indentation.
  - ☐ quotation marks.
  - ☐ internal punctuation.

Grammar & Mechanics

- ☐ I looked over my pie
  - ☐ names of people
  - ☐ places.
  - ☐ brand names.
- ☐ I reviewed my verb t
  - ☐ my verb tenses
  - ☐ my verb endings

Punctuation

- ☐ I considered my ending punctuation, making sure that:
  - ☐ there is ending punctuation.
  - ☐ it creates the tone I want for that part.
- ☐ I read my piece aloud, listening for the sound of my sentences, considering:
  - ☐ if I may need commas to slow down parts.
  - ☐ if any internal punctuation may be missing.

Digital Tools

- ☐ I used a digital tool such as spell and grammar check or an AI editing review, and as I did so, I was careful to:
  - ☐ review suggestions.
  - ☐ maintain my voice and the voice of any characters.
  - ☐ cite AI support in a footnote, endnote, or acknowledgment.

Lesson 1

(Tucking in Secrets)

STRATEGY

Writers, especially narrative writers, know that parentheticals allow the writer to tuck in extra information and compose sentences that are enticing. Often, writers consider including secrets about a character, details about a setting, or a backstory.

Visit hs-guidetoteaching.org to access a collection of parentheticals.

USE THIS STRATEGY...to intrigue your students into caring about conventions and to introduce a sentence structure that is enticing and effective.

Inquiry Question

How do writers use parentheses to tuck in secrets about characters? Where might I try this in my writing?

Parentheses Practice

Chris (whom I had adored since we were eight) walked slowly toward us.

Chris (laughing blue eyes, wild golden hair, sun-kissed brown skin) walked slowly toward us.

Chris (who had briefly dated Lisa two years ago) walked slowly toward us.

Chris (who had briefly dated Lisa and whose feelings for Lisa I still worried about) walked slowly toward us.

Chris (the fastest boy in New York State) walked slowly toward us.

Chris (who had already won his race, making him not only the fastest boy in New York but now in the nation) walked slowly toward us.

I turned toward Lisa (my best friend since kindergarten).

I turned toward Lisa (my closest competitor in this race).

I turned toward Lisa (long brown hair, longer legs, cool brown eyes).

I turned toward Lisa (who had eyes only for Chris, today and every day).

I turned toward Lisa (whom I loved and feared in equal measure).

I turned toward Lisa (her long sleeves covering the bruises on her arm, and her makeup covering the exhaustion in her face).

LAUNCH THE INQUIRY

- Suggest to students that writers seek sentence structures that are enticing. Introduce the inquiry question, and explain that parentheticals are sentences where the writer tucks secrets into the parenthesis. In narrative writing, these are usually secrets about the character.
- Invite students to explore a collection of sentences with parentheticals. We return to one of our familiar teacher demonstration texts where we experimented with multiple parentheticals. You could easily create your own collection!
- Suggest that students work with a partner to explore the inquiry question, asking what kinds of secrets are tucked into the parenthesis in some of these sentences.
- You might collect some of their responses, namely that writers use parentheses to tuck in details about characters' backstory, their appearance, relationships, and how the writer feels about the character.

- Invite writers to try this work in their memoir, finding places where they can insert parentheticals as a way to tuck in details and secrets about characters and, if they want to expand this work, secrets about places.

PROMPTS TO COACH STUDENTS AND PARTNERSHIPS

Usually, you insert parentheses right after a character's name, and you tuck details inside the parentheses that aren't in the sentence.

You can also set off secrets with commas (these are called appositives), or dashes.

You can also add parentheses after a place, to give unusual details about the setting.

- Lisa and I sat in the stadium stands (where I thought Chris would kiss me, in one longing moment in seventh grade) …
- Lisa and I sat in the stadium stands (mostly empty, because nobody really cared about track) …

CLASSROOM ARTIFACTS

We rode our bikes to DQ (dripping cones, sticky hands, desperate crushes), every day that summer.

Amber (chess queen, math whiz, and the hottest girl in eleventh grade) glanced at me in calculus.

Savaria's mother stood by the grave (in which her daughter lay, alone, under the dirt).

Julia—mi mejor amiga—was waiting for me on her steps.

Sarah, who sat ahead of me in math, unbraided her long, gleaming hair and let it fall down her back.

Students revise with parenthesis, tucking in information and secrets about characters and places.

Lesson 2

Punctuating Dialogue: An Inquiry

Visit hs-guidetoteaching.org to access an excerpt from The Hate U Give by Angie Thomas and a tool for a student-led inquiry.

STRATEGY

Writers know that punctuating dialogue can be tricky, even for experienced writers. One way writers remind themselves of these conventions is by studying published writers. They zoom in on dialogue tags, quotation marks, commas, and other punctuation marks, asking: What can I learn from published writers about the norms of dialogue?

USE THIS STRATEGY...to remind students that they can use any mentor to study and learn about how to punctuate and format dialogue, and to support students in learning the intricacies of punctuating dialogue.

Inquiry Question

What can we learn from published writers about how to punctuate dialogue?

LAUNCH THE INQUIRY

- Explain to students that the conventions for punctuating dialogue are complicated, and that as soon as writers start using dialogue, they'll want to investigate what they can learn from published writers.
- Introduce the inquiry question and a text to study. We use an easy and engaging text with varied dialogue, in this case, an excerpt from *The Hate U Give* (2017). Of course, you can also use any text that you're studying or that's in your classroom library.

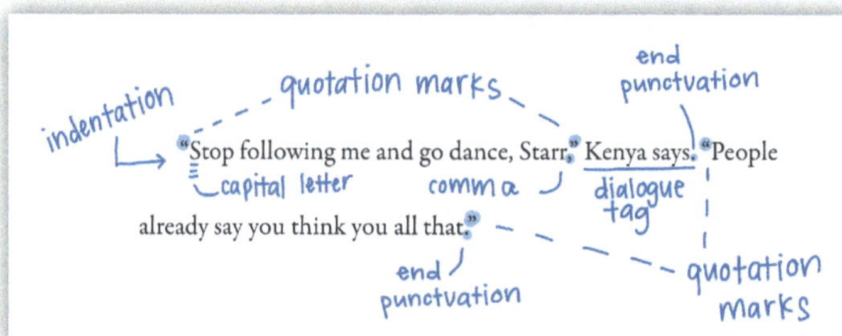

When Lauren did this work with her class, she studied a few pages from the start of *The Hate U Give* with her students, to help them notice all the small details of punctuating dialogue. As Lauren annotated an excerpt, she helped her students notice the internal punctuation and capitalization.

- Invite students to work with a partner to mark up an excerpt from the text and then to share what they've learned about punctuating dialogue.
- While this information is in the forefront of their thinking, and with their mentor text in hand, have students return to their own memoirs to find any dialogue and to work on punctuating it wisely. They might also revise to add dialogue tags, split dialogue, and delete some dialogue tags.

PROMPTS TO COACH STUDENTS AND PARTNERSHIPS

The simplest way to let your reader know who is talking is to insert a dialogue tag, like "he said/yelled/cried/whispered."

Sometimes authors skip dialogue tags, when it's easy to figure out who is speaking.

Split dialogue, when you put a dialogue tag in the middle of a sentence, is especially tricky. Check, because usually the first word after the dialogue tag isn't capitalized, unless it is someone's name.

CLASSROOM ARTIFACTS

Punctuating Dialogue: Inquiry Station

Welcome!
The Hate U Give will teach you how to make your dialogue more sophisticated... and how to punctuate it.

Step 1	Read pages 4–5. With your partner, list what you can learn from Angie Thomas about dialogue that you can try in your writing. (How does she let the reader know who is talking? What's interesting and tricky?)
Step 2	Now review, "The Terminology of Dialogue," clarifying any components that are causing confusion.
Step 3	With your partner, look at pages 4–5 and talk again about what you can learn from Angie Thomas about dialogue including how to punctuate it. Use the Terminology of Dialogue chart to support. (Hint: What puncutation goes inside or outside the quotation marks?)
Step 4	Extra challenge. Study the dialogue below, name the moves and try them out in your own writing. "And it wouldn't kill you not to dress like..." Kenya turns up her nose as she looks from my sneakers to my oversized hoodie. "That. Ain't that my brother's hoodie?"

The Terminology of Dialogue

Dialogue Tags	Phrases that tell you who is talking. Ex: She said, called, cried, yelled.
Quotation Marks	The " " marks go outside what people say. Ex: "Stop following me and go dance."
Commas	These usually come just before the quotation marks. Ex: Starr mumbled, "Whatever." Sometimes they come at the end if the dialogue tag is after. Ex: "Whatever," Starr mumbled.
Capital Letters	Mark the beginning of new dialogue. Ex: "Hey, I'm just saying," Kenya said
Exclamation Marks & Question Marks	These are usually at the end of the dialogue and they usually come just before the final quotation mark. Ex: Do I look like I care what people think?" Starr asked.
Indentations	Dialogue usually starts on a new line and paragraph, indented.

Creating an inquiry station, or center, allows students to investigate conventions with independence.

Lesson 3

Narrative Paragraphing

STRATEGY

Writers know that there are no rules about when to paragraph in stories, but there are opportunities, including to use paragraphs to introduce new characters, places, or times; to call attention to new information; and for dramatic effect.

Visit hs-guidetoteaching.org to download a sample text with and without paragraphs.

USE THIS STRATEGY...as soon as students are writing long stretches of narrative. This strategy can also help writers think of their writing in parts. (Note, in this lesson we have not included new paragraphs to mark dialogue, since we visited that concept in Lesson 2: Punctuating Dialogue.)

The Backseat — / = new paragraph

Lisa and I sat in the backseat of her brother John's Camaro. The windows of the car shook with the sound of the warm-up band. Inside, it was steamy. / We had won tickets to the concert on the radio. We had called in to Kiss FM and answered a series of trivia questions about Grease - the name of the high school (Rydell), the leader of the Pink Ladies (Rizzo), the name of the beauty school Frenchie drops out of (National Beauty School), and the TV dance show that comes to Rydell (National Bandstand). We knew all things there were to know about Grease. / Last Halloween, Lisa went to school as Sandy (not dainty and demure Sandy but Sandy from 'You're the One that I Want,' in black hotpants and strapless top and heels). Our school had never seen anything like that, and when Principal Hodge saw Lisa in the hall he dropped his cigarette in the trashcan, called her dad, and sent her home early. / It was (they said) the Rolling Stones' last tour. Lisa and I were only in ninth grade, and our moms wouldn't let us go alone. But they let us go with John and Brian. John, who had led the high school football team to the state championship. John, who had been the youngest Eagle Scout in our town. Brian, who was captain of our school hockey team, who also had a temper, who sometimes we were afraid of. / John lit something in the front seat. Something smoky...and sweet... He passed it to Brian, who reached towards us, offering it. I knew what it was. Marijuana. Pot. My mom had explained about it. The gateway drug. A straight path from there to crystal meth. A slow slide into addiction, street life, possibly prostitution. / Lisa leaned over to whisper in my ear. She whispered fiercely that I shouldn't embarrass her.

TEACH THE STRATEGY

- Suggest to your writers that narrative writers know that there are no rules about when to paragraph, but if they think as readers, they realize that readers really appreciate paragraphs, especially when new characters, settings, and times are introduced.
- Invite writers to join you in studying part of a narrative, asking the question: Where could I insert paragraphs, and why? You might print the excerpt from Mary's piece "The Backseat" for partners to mark up.

When Mary did this with her class, she shared an excerpt that she had drafted deliberately to include shifts in time, characters, and tone. She invited students to work in partnerships, talking about where they would insert paragraphs, and why. Getting kids to talk about conventions as craft, and to have meaningful conversations about conventions, is one of the goals here.

- Share a chart as a reminder for writers of when narrative writers might paragraph.
- Invite students to do similar work in their memoirs, rereading, asking themselves: Where do I see opportunities for paragraphs?

PROMPTS TO COACH STUDENTS AND PARTNERSHIPS

It helps to read thinking of your audience: Where would a reader appreciate a paragraph? Remember, too, that readers appreciate white space. You can even think about your spacing between paragraphs.

Anytime something changes, readers like to be alerted, and a paragraph helps them pay attention.

You might have other reasons to paragraph as well, like if you are shifting to reflection, or you are inserting dialogue. Look at your mentor texts for when they paragraph.

Lesson 3 (Continued)

CLASSROOM ARTIFACTS

Everything changes when you find out Santa isn't real. Something about Christmas just isn't the same anymore when someone breaks the awful news to you or when you figure it out yourself. In my case, people accidentally told me multiple times before I figured out it was all a lie. The first, and most memorable, time I heard the news I was sitting on the couch wit[h] sister watching a documentary about mermaids when my aunt laughed: "Merm[aids] just like Santa". I remember thinking she was so stupid and walking up to my [mom] her what she said. *How could someone disrespect Santa Claus like that?!* The[n] fourth grade as I was eating my after-school snack it just hit me that Santa Cla[us] Elf-On-The-Shelf were never real. Everything was a lie. Running downstairs morning to look for Timmy the elf on the shelf was a lie. The fat man in red [g] was a lie. Christmas was a lie.

Everything changes when you find out Santa isn't real. Something about Christmas just isn't the same anymore when someone breaks the awful news to you or when you figure it out yourself.

In my case, people accidentally told me multiple times before I figured out it was all a lie. The first, and most memorable, time I heard the news I was sitting on the couch with my aunt and sister watching a documentary about mermaids when my aunt laughed: "Mermaids aren't real just like Santa". I remember thinking she was so stupid and walking up to my mom and telling her what she said. *How could someone disrespect Santa Claus like that?!*

Then one day, in the fourth grade as I was eating my after-school snack it just hit me that Santa Claus and the Elf-On-The-Shelf were never real. Everything was a lie. Running downstairs every December morning to look for Timmy the elf on the shelf was a lie.The fat man in red giving me presents was a lie. Christmas was a lie.

Everything changes when you find out Santa isn't real. Something about Christmas just isn't the same anymore when someone breaks the awful news to you or when you figure it out yourself.

In my case, people accidentally told me multiple times before I figured out it was all a lie. The first, and most memorable, time I heard the news I was sitting on the couch with my aunt and sister watching a documentary about mermaids when my aunt laughed: "Mermaids aren't real just like Santa". I remember thinking she was so stupid and walking up to my mom and telling her what she said.

How could someone disrespect Santa Claus like that?!

Then one day, in the fourth grade as I was eating my after-school snack it just hit me that Santa Claus and the Elf-On-The-Shelf were never real.

Everything was a lie.

Running downstairs every December morning to look for Timmy the elf on the shelf was a lie.

The fat man in red giving me presents was a lie.

Christmas was a lie.

This narrative writer tries paragraphing part of her memoir two different ways.

Mimetic Sentence Writing

Lesson 4

STRATEGY

Writers often engage in mimetic writing, that is, crafting sentences using mentor sentences from published writers as direct inspiration. Mirroring interesting sentence structures gives writers surprising vitality in their own sentences.

USE THIS STRATEGY...to introduce a variety of more complex sentence structures to your writers, and to inculcate in them the method of mentoring themselves to published writers, including at the sentence level.

Visit hs-guidetoteaching.org to download a collection of mentor sentences.

TEACH THE STRATEGY

- Explain to your students what mimetic writing is: mentoring yourself at the sentence level to a published writer, mirroring their exact syntax, or sentence structure, and substituting your content, to try out more complicated and intriguing sentence structures.
- Introduce a collection of mentor sentences.
- Model how you choose a couple of mentor sentences and mirror-write, weaving in your own content from your memoir. Sometimes it helps to tap the parts of the mentor sentence and circle the punctuation.

Mirror Sentence Writing

And so we beat on, boats against the current, borne back ceaselessly into the past.

F. Scott Fitzgerald, *The Great Gatsby*

Still we swam with the tides, our bodies floated through saltwater, carried softly and endlessly toward memories we made in the waves.

My house. My chair. My woman.

Rebecca Yarros, *Iron Flame*

My ocean. My beach. My sanctuary.

When Coley modeled this work, she chose two mentor sentences, including one whose style she loved but whose content she did not, and wove her own content into the same syntax, using her memoir topic.

You'll find you don't have to coach this work as much as you might predict—young people often have an acute sense of matching patterns.

- Encourage students to select a series of mentor sentences to try this with. After they've drafted some sentences, encourage them to consider revising that part of their memoir to situate the content of the sentence.

PROMPTS TO COACH STUDENTS AND PARTNERSHIPS

Sometimes you can take a sentence or two you've already written and redraft them, mirroring the mentor exactly.

When you mirror-write, it's also okay to make most of it the same and change one part; that can also lead to interesting sentences.

Often you'll find yourself mirroring the tone and content, which can lead to new surprises in your own writing.

CLASSROOM ARTIFACTS

My very photogenic mother died in a freak accident (picnic, lightning) when I was three.
Vladimir Nabakov, *Lolita*

My ridiculously clumsy brother broke my arm (lightsaber, fight scene)

when I was twelve.

Home, where she longed to be, where she and her mother could be warm together, was far behind.

William Steig, *Brave Irene*

Camp, where she fit in, where her awkwardness and loneliness could disappear, was lost to her now.

As Estha stirred the thick jam he thought Two Thoughts and the Two Thoughts he thought were these: a) Anything can happen to anyone. and b) It is best to be prepared.
Arundhati Roy, *The God of Small Things*

As Evan put away his lacrosse stick he thought Three Thoughts and the Three Thoughts he thought were these: a) Anyone can accidentally score for the other team and b) He needed to switch high schools and c) It wasn't his idea to play lacrosse.

Mimetic writing leads to artful and surprising sentences, and sometimes new content.

The Magic of Verbs

Lesson 5

STRATEGY

Writers know that verbs anchor writing, in terms of establishing time and action, and shifts in either of these. It can be helpful for writers to study mentor texts, investigating how authors experimented with verbs. They pay attention to the tense, the verb endings, and the precision of the words. Then, they carry these same lenses to their own writing as they revise their verbs.

USE THIS STRATEGY...during the revision and editing process to encourage students to audit and change their verbs in their own writing and to set the stage for coaching students around verb tense, as needed.

Visit hs-guidetoteaching.org to access a sample excerpt and teaching chart.

TEACH THE STRATEGY

- Suggest to your writers that verbs often anchor writing, especially in terms of establishing time and action, and also tone. Introduce lenses for studying verbs using the following chart.
- Invite writers to study a mentor text, noticing the verb tense, the endings of the verbs, and the specificity of the words chosen. We used an excerpt from *Educated* by Tara Westover (2018).
- Annotate the passage focusing on what students noticed about the verbs.

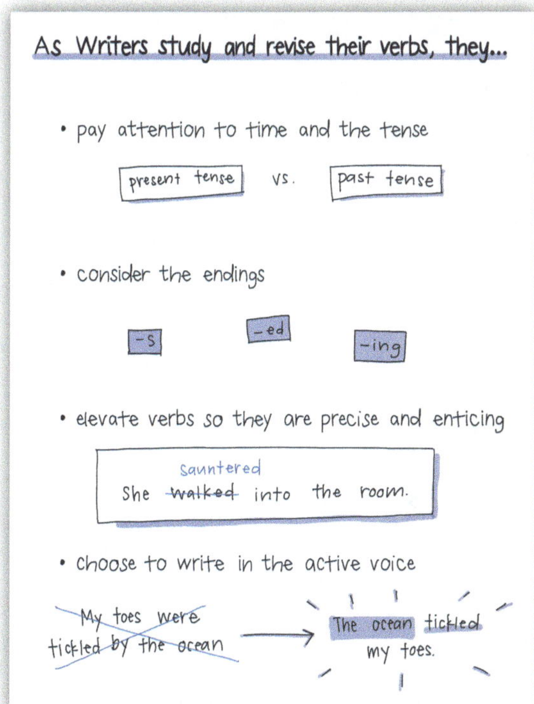

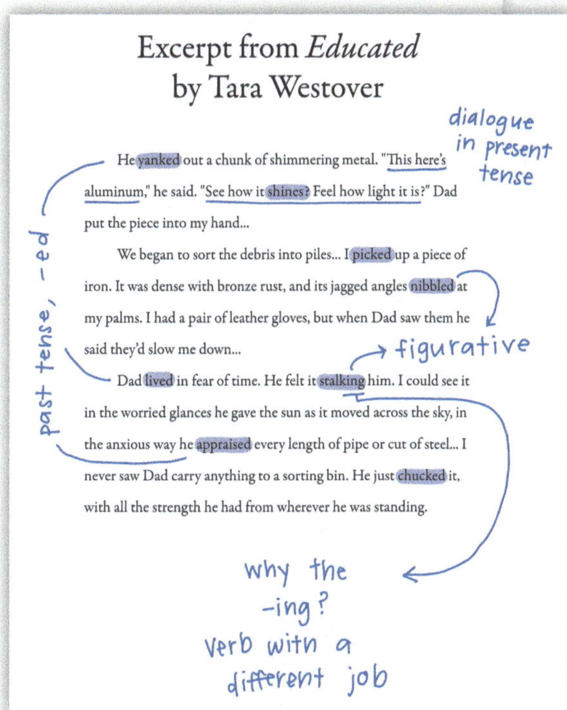

Excerpt from *Educated*
by Tara Westover

He yanked out a chunk of shimmering metal. "This here's aluminum," he said. "See how it shines? Feel how light it is?" Dad put the piece into my hand...

We began to sort the debris into piles... I picked up a piece of iron. It was dense with bronze rust, and its jagged angles nibbled at my palms. I had a pair of leather gloves, but when Dad saw them he said they'd slow me down...

Dad lived in fear of time. He felt it stalking him. I could see it in the worried glances he gave the sun as it moved across the sky, in the anxious way he appraised every length of pipe or cut of steel... I never saw Dad carry anything to a sorting bin. He just chucked it, with all the strength he had from wherever he was standing.

Lesson 5 (Continued)

- Model this work with your own writing, showcasing how you highlight your verbs and then check in on the tense, voice, and precision of the verbs (see Classroom Artifacts for an example).
- Send students off to highlight the verbs in their own writing, looking for patterns and places to elevate their words, maintain a consistent tense, and prioritize active voice.

PROMPTS TO COACH STUDENTS AND PARTNERSHIPS

You can also do this work with other parts of speech like nouns or adjectives, asking yourself if you've selected the "just right" word for this moment. Often, you want to be more precise, rather than less.

Poetry is a great place to study verbs as poets are very conscious of their word count. You might try looking through our collection of poems and studying the verbs.

Experiment with multiple words until you get the right one. Notice how, in the examples, some of the words are unlikely in the context, like metal "nibbling" or the sun "stalking."

CLASSROOM ARTIFACTS

The Race

Even as I ran, I ~~remembered~~ recollected Chris and Lisa, and how ~~connected~~ entangled we were. I remembered when Chris arrived on our block. He was eight years old and beautiful in a way that would ~~change~~ unsettle our neighborhood forever. Lisa made brownies to celebrate, but when she ~~gave~~ gifted me one through the chain-link fence that separated our back yards, and I put it in my mouth, it was made of mud. I felt ~~full of~~ soaked with betrayal.

I remembered playing tackle tag in Mrs. Terhaar's yard. How Lisa and I would sprint, ~~getting away from~~ evading all others, ~~slowing down~~ decelerating just ahead of Chris. How he would lower you gently to the ground, his arms ~~around~~ circling your back. How all I would ever know about desire I learned playing tackle tag in fourth grade, on Mrs. Terhaar's lawn.

When Mary modeled this work, she invited her students to help her sharpen her verbs, choosing ones that were more literary, more specific, and occasionally metaphoric.

Zoming in on Parts of Speech

Lesson 6

STRATEGY

Writers elevate their vocabulary and sentences in revision. One way to do this work is to pay attention to parts of speech, especially those that involve actions and descriptions. Specifically, writers can study a memoir in parts, asking which part of speech needs to be specific and enticing in this part?

USE THIS STRATEGY...to encourage students to be more precise and specific in their word choice; to push students to think about the main function of each part of their memoir; when students are editing and close to the end of the writing process.

Visit hs-guidetoteaching.org to download a collection of memoir excerpts.

TEACH THE STRATEGY

- Suggest to your writers that to elevate their vocabulary and sentences is to pay attention to parts of speech, especially those that involve actions and descriptions.
- Introduce the idea that in each section of our writing, different parts of speech are most important, thinking about how adjectives and nouns are most important in scenes that describe people while places and verbs are most important when there is action.
    - For a lesson specifically about verbs and time, go to Chapter 2, Lesson 3, and for revising verb choices, go to Lesson 5 in this chapter.

Use Parts of Speech Strategically

Focus on verbs to...	Zoom in on nouns to...	Use adjectives to...
• Anchor the reader in time • Build tension or emotion • Reveal indirect information about a character	• Establish people, places, or objects that matter • Name emotions indirectly • Weave in symbols	• Slow down a moment • Develop a mood/tone • Describe a setting or character

- Invite writers to study a few mentor texts, deciding which part of speech is most powerful in each one, highlighting the words that are most precise and enticing (see examples of annotated texts below, in Classroom Artifacts).
- Coach students to pick a section of their memoir, decide the part of speech most important to that section, and work to make those words enticing and precise.
- Remind students that all parts of speech matter in each part, that this is just an exercise to get them to zoom into their words with a lens. Encourage students to return to their overall revision work, with this as an additional lens.

Lesson 6
(Continued)

PROMPTS TO COACH STUDENTS AND PARTNERSHIPS

Remember that all parts of speech are important throughout, so you can also think of this as just being more precise and enticing in your diction.

Poetry is a great place to study diction as poets are very conscious of their word choice. You might try looking through our collection of poems and studying the diction, pulling words you might use in your own writing.

Experiment with multiple words until you get the right one. Notice how, in the examples, some of the words are unlikely in the context, like "nibbling" or "stalking."

CLASSROOM ARTIFACTS

Excerpt from *Crying in H Mart* by Michelle Zauner

Ever since my mom died, I cry in H Mart.

H Mart is a supermarket chain that specializes in Asian food. The H stands for **han ah reum, a Korean phrase** that roughly translates to **"one arm** full of **groceries."** H Mart is where parachute kids flock to find the **brand of instant noodles** that reminds them of home. It's where Korean families buy rice cakes to make **tteokguk, the beef and rice cake soup** that brings in **the New Year.** It's the only place where you can find a giant **vat of peeled garlic,** because it's the only place that truly understands how much garlic you'll need for the kind of food your people eat. H Mart is freedom from the single-aisle "ethnic" section of regular grocery stores. They don't prop **Goya Beans** next to **bottles of sriracha** here.

Excerpt from *Becoming* by Michelle Obama

If you've never passed a winter in Chicago, let me describe it: You can live for **a hundred straight** days beneath the **iron-gray** sky that claps itself **like a lid** over the city. **Frigid, biting** winds blow in off the lake. Snow falls in dozens of ways, in **heavy overnight** dumps and **daytime sweeping** squalls, in **demoralizing sloppy** sleet and **fairy-tale** billows of fluff. There's ice, usually, lots of it, that shellacks the sidewalks and windshields that then needs to be scraped. There's the sound of the scraping in the morning—the hack, hack, hack of it–as people clear their cars to go to work. Your neighbors, **unrecognizable** in the **thick** layers they wear against the cold, keep their faces down to avoid the wind.

Excerpt from *Educated* by Tara Westover

He **yanked** out a chunk of shimmering metal. "This here's aluminum," he said. "See how it **shines**? **Feel** how light it is?" Dad put the piece into my hand...

We began to sort the debris into piles...I picked up a piece of iron. It was dense with bronze rust, and its jagged angles **nibbled** at my palms. I had a pair of leather gloves, but when dad saw them he said they'd slow me down....

Dad lived in fear of time. He felt it **stalking** him. I could see it in the worried glances he **gave** the sun as it moved across the sky, in the anxious way he **appraised** every length of pipe or cut of steel...I never saw Dad carry anything to a sorting bin. He just **chucked** it, with all the strength he said from wherever he was standing.

Annotating mentors for different parts of speech.

Ending Punctuation Creates ... Tone!

Lesson 7

STRATEGY

Writers know that punctuation guides how readers hear sentences as they read. Knowing this, they return to key sentences and experiment with punctuation that will create the tone the writer aims for.

USE THIS STRATEGY...to help your writers add ending punctuation more purposefully and to help them play with tone shifts in parts of their piece.

Visit hs-guidetoteaching.org to download a "Snow Day" poem ready for students to add punctuation.

TEACH THE STRATEGY

- Suggest to your writers that punctuation does more than make sentences understandable; it affects the tone of voice the reader imagines and the overall tone and meaning of that part of the text.
- Introduce a text without punctuation (we use a small excerpt about a possible snow day), and invite students to join you in adding punctuation to create different tones.

When Lauren taught this lesson, she and her students played with different punctuation to create a tone of uncertainty or one of joy, familiar feelings for any teachers or students who have longed for snow days.

- Invite students to look back over their pieces and consider what tone they want in certain parts, and to play with their sentences and ending punctuation accordingly.

PROMPTS TO COACH STUDENTS AND PARTNERSHIPS

Try reading aloud a sentence or two, with different punctuation choices—or ask your partner to—and listen for what you prefer.

Sometimes it's interesting to draft new sentences and play with ellipses and other punctuation as a way of creating new parts.

It's fun to try different punctuation at the end, but some of these marks are for the middle of sentences. Try playing with the dash, the ellipses, or the semicolon.

CLASSROOM ARTIFACTS

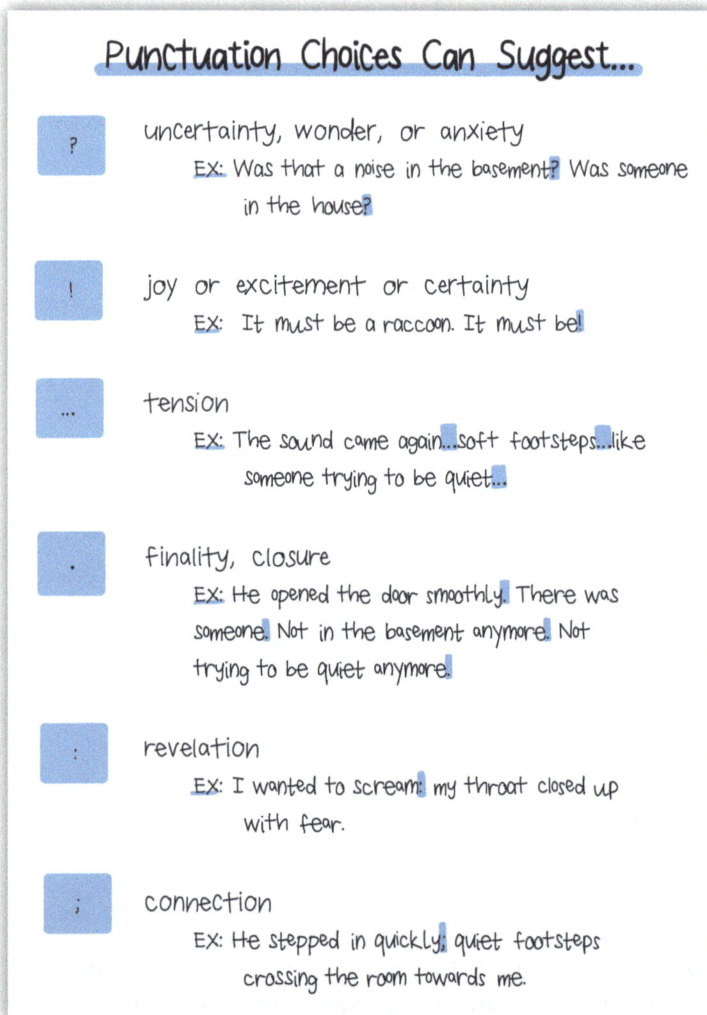

Punctuation Choices Can Suggest...

? uncertainty, wonder, or anxiety
EX: Was that a noise in the basement? Was someone in the house?

! joy or excitement or certainty
EX: It must be a raccoon. It must be!

... tension
EX: The sound came again...soft footsteps...like someone trying to be quiet...

. finality, closure
EX: He opened the door smoothly. There was someone. Not in the basement anymore. Not trying to be quiet anymore.

: revelation
EX: I wanted to scream: my throat closed up with fear.

; connection
EX: He stepped in quickly; quiet footsteps crossing the room towards me.

A classroom tool to help writers revise punctuation to create tone.

Once it became a little darker outside and the sun set, we all would play hide and go seek tag. It was terrifying to say the least, hiding behind bushes with thorns threatening to scratch you, scraping your knees attempting to hide under cars. Getting spotted and dashing away to the next planned hiding spot was the most nerve wracking part. Running away until your lungs couldn't handle it, heart thumping loudly against your chest made us feel young and alive.

Once it became a little darker outside and the sun set, we all would play hide and go seek tag. It was terrifying to say the least: hiding behind bushes with thorns threatening to scratch you, scraping your knees attempting to hide under cars. Getting spotted and dashing away to the next planned hiding spot was the most nerve wracking part! Running away until your lungs couldn't handle it? Heart thumping loudly against your chest ~~made us feel~~ ? It reminded us that we are young and alive . . .

This writer experiments with adding different types of punctuation in her memoir.

Lesson 8

Using AI Translation Wisely and Ethically

STRATEGY

When narrative writers turn to AI for translation support, they know it's important to train the AI partner to sustain the writer's voice and style as well as to sustain character's idioms, *and* it's important to reference AI use in a simple and transparent way, such as a footnote or acknowledgment.

USE THIS STRATEGY...to especially help multilingual students and newcomers use translation tools wisely—and avoid trouble by referencing this use. Know that students who feel insecure in the classroom language will turn to AI, and they desperately need instruction on how to train AI as a partner and how to use it ethically in school.

Visit hs-guidetoteaching.org to download a Dos and Don'ts of AI Translation chart.

TEACH THE STRATEGY

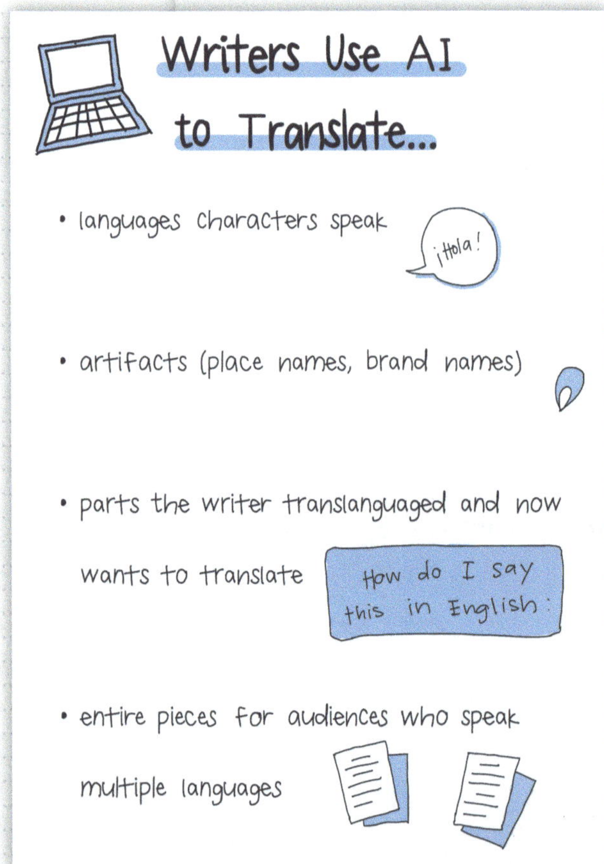

- Explain to students that professionals turn to AI for translation support often, and they've learned some tips, both for training their AI partner and for referencing it.
- Invite students to talk with a partner about when they could imagine wanting AI to translate something for them as writers. You might collect students' ideas in a quick chart.
- Demonstrate how you might use and reference AI for translation support, as shown in the Classroom Artifacts next.
- Introduce a chart of Dos and Don'ts for AI Translations, and invite students to study it with a partner, talking about what part seems most relevant to them as writers.
- Invite students to consider what part of their memoir—or in certain circumstances, their whole memoir—they might want to translate, and if so, how they would train their AI partner and reference their AI support.

Do's and Dont's with AI Translation

Do...	Because...
Ask AI to translate words, phrases, and lines that you can write most powerfully in one language, and want to convey in a second language.	Translanguaging (reaching for your most powerful language) to express yourself is powerful, and AI can help translate this power.

Don't...	Because...
Ask AI to translate an entire piece for you without training your AI to mirror your voice, style, content and/or informing readers that the piece has been translated by AI.	AI will translate in a way that overwrites and changes your voice, style, and often content, so that you are no longer the primary author of the piece, but are now a co-author.

Do...	Because...
Train your AI partner by uploading pieces in all the languages you write. Ask it to study your language, voice, idioms, and style, and to use these pieces as mentor texts when supporting you as a writing partner.	AI can learn about you as a writer, and work inside parameters you set, especially by studying your writing, so that it holds itself as a writing partner to your writing voice.

Don't...	Because...
Expect that it will go unnoticed when AI does sweeping translations for you.	When translating, AI both elevates language and produces some rough parts —both of which are noticeable

Do...	Because...
Read over any translated material very closely, and if possible ask another fluent human to read and revise.	Sometimes AI gets part of a translation wrong, or misunderstands an idiom, and/or translates word-for-word in a way that is awkward.

PROMPTS TO COACH STUDENTS AND PARTNERSHIPS

If you translate a large section or a whole piece, you can try to check the idioms and overall flow by asking for help from someone who is fluent, or using a different translation app, like DeepL, and then comparing translations. Expect there will be some rough patches, and reference AI support clearly so your audience expects this.

One way to reference AI support is with a simple footnote that says, "This author received support in translation from an AI partner, on (this date)." You can also add: "Translation was only for (part or paragraph or line)," or "This author trained her AI partner using her own writing, to maintain her content and language choices."

If you're unsure about translation and what you're allowed to do, talk to a teacher and possibly a counselor, being sure to let them know why you want to translate.

CLASSROOM ARTIFACTS

Please translate this dialogue into Italian. The grandmother in the story was from Sardinia, and I want the dialogue to be accurate to her roots. The dialogue is: We walked into Lisa's kitchen and the smell of baked seadas – a kind of fried pastry filled with cheese, and drizzled with honey. Lisa's Nonna was making culurgiones. She patted Lisa's hair, saying, "Sit, darling, eat! You're too skinny!"

We walked into Lisa's kitchen and the smell of baked seadas - a kind of fried pastry filled with cheese, and drizzled with honey. Lisa's Nonna was making culurgiones. She patted Lisa's hair, saying, "Assèdati, figgia mia, mangia! Ses troppo magra!"

...

*ChatGPT helped with seeking Sardinian dialect and translation.

-OR-

Acknowledgements

I'd like to thank Lisa's Nonna for all the delicious Sardinian meals she cooked us, and thank ChatGPT for support with the translation in this piece, especially of Sardinian dialect.

Mary shows students how to ask an AI partner to translate dialogue, so it matches the language of the character in her story. She also shows two ways to include a reference at the end of the narrative.

How to Train, Learn from, and Reference an AI Editor

Lesson 9

STRATEGY

Increasingly, writers turn to AI for editing support. As they use AI, they quickly realize it's important to train an AI partner to personalize its feedback. It's also important to learn *from* their AI partner, so writers become a more skilled writer/editor. Finally, it's always important to reference AI support.

USE THIS STRATEGY...to help your writers learn wise ways with AI, especially avoiding letting AI overwrite their pieces, and to help your writers become more confident with referencing AI.

Visit hs-guidetoteaching.org to access a teaching chart on training AI as a personal editor.

TEACH THE STRATEGY

- Remind students that digital editing tools can be very helpful, that writers almost always turn to these before sharing any high-stakes writing, and that AI is so powerful that it changes the ways we interact with digital editors.
- Explain to students that many writers turn to AI to support the editing process, but that because AI is so powerful, it works differently than tools such as the spell and grammar checks in Google Docs or Microsoft Word. AI will do a sweeping revision inside of an edit, in ways that can overwrite and distort the original writer's voice, style, and even content.
- Suggest that it's important to train your AI partner, especially by providing samples of your writing, and to reference AI support. It's also important to read its suggestions carefully and reject those that don't fit your goals and style.
- Model this process for students with your own writing. Introduce the chart, How to Train Your AI Personal Editor and Learn from It, to reinforce the steps you go through. See the model under Classroom Artifacts.

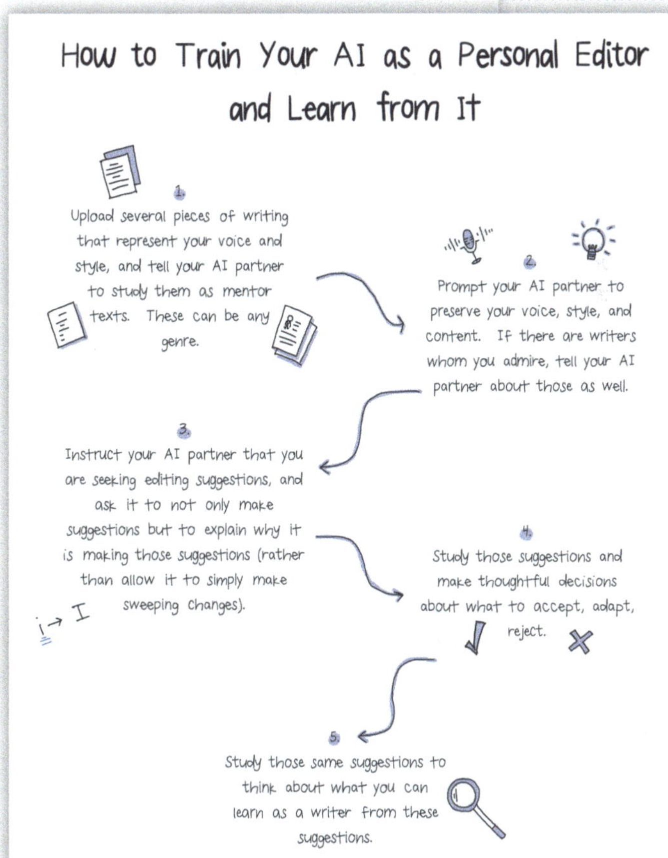

- Encourage students to try this work in their own writing.

PROMPTS TO COACH STUDENTS AND PARTNERSHIPS

It helps to tell your AI partner to not change any dialogue, as a way to preserve the idioms and sound of your characters.

When you train your AI partner, share pieces in multiple genres. It can get to know you as a writer by studying your poetry, your essays, your stories—any writing you like that highlights your voice.

You can reference AI support by a simple footnote at the end: "ChatGPT version 5.0 supported editing for conventions. I trained it not to interfere with my voice or style or content."

CLASSROOM ARTIFACTS

I'm writing a story about going to the beach with my mom. Here's an excerpt from my writing. Could you provide some editing feedback? What grammatical changes might I want to make? Spelling? Sentence structure? The beach has always been ours. Whether I was six or sixteen, my mom and I always found our way to the beach together. I remember loving the water and jumping in with my colorful water shoes. I'd always say, "Mom, mom, watch me go all the way under" which really meant let me stick half my face in the water and ask her if I went down realllllllly deep. She's my mom, so of course she said, "Yes." everytime

It was always a good day if we were at the beach, but there were a few....mishaps? Maybe that's the right word? I was a pretty friendly child and across the day I'd wander over to people's blankets scoping out their food. I'd wander over and make some small talk or just dive right in with the punchline. "Hi, I'm Colwey. Can I have some gwapes?" There were too many times to count that she found me on other people's blankets eating and laughing with them

Copy of Ice Cream_ A Memoir (1).pdf
PDF

Free Write Kat ML.pdf
PDF

Please use these texts, which I've written, as mentor texts, so that as you make editing suggestions, you maintain my voice, word choice, and style.

Coley shares a snippet of her story with her AI partner and asks for feedback.

Suggested Edits & Why:

1. **"everytime" → "Every time"**
   → "Every time" should be two words.
2. **Dialogue punctuation and capitalization**
   → Capitalized "Mom" in the quote and added a punctuation mark for natural speech rhythm: "Mom, Mom, watch me go all the way under!"
   → Also added an em dash and italics for "really" to keep your tone but improve readability.
3. **Ellipses and spacing**
   → Changed "....mishaps?" to "... mishaps?" for a cleaner, more standard look. Three dots is the usual convention for ellipses.
4. **Sentence clarity and punctuation**
   → Smoothed out some of the longer or run-on sentences for flow, e.g.,:
   - "across the day I'd wander over..." → "throughout the day, I'd wander over..."
   - "eating and laughing with them" → added a comma before "eating" to improve rhythm.
5. **Optional for effect**
   → You could italicize "gwapes" to emphasize the adorable childhood pronunciation.

Coley's AI partner explains its suggestions so she can learn from these tips.

Chapter Five: Exploring Publishing Modalities

Publishing our writing is an important part of the writing process for all writers. Oftentimes young writers see "publishing" as turning in their drafts for a grade. While that's part of writing for school, we also want to show them that publishing can be joyful and reflective. It's also the point where you have to declare you are finished, that this writing is done for the moment. Here, we want to both encourage students to be okay with the finality of their drafts, but also encourage that, ultimately, they can keep tinkering with the piece of writing, or that it might become something bigger. Mostly, we want to inspire our students to share their writing with real audiences.

This chapter starts, as most of our chapters do, by studying mentor texts as inspiration. Studying these mentors allows for kids to dream up all the possibilities of memoir, beyond the typed document in front of them. After this study, some students might want to publish their memoirs as picture books, podcasts, graphic novels, or even videos. It can be natural to feel a little uncomfortable with this if you aren't familiar with all the technology or skills needed to make it happen. This is a great opportunity to let kids lead and teach each other. In Lesson 2, you'll find a sample sign-up sheet for student-run lessons. Kids can teach each other about how to use software or even the language of a medium. They often know more than we do, so our role becomes to *facilitate* the leadership and the teaching. You could also have kids partner up, where one illustrates the other's writing. We've seen teachers partner their writers with the art or graphic design classes.

If you've been on this journey alongside us, you know we are embracing AI as a classroom tool. The lesson in this chapter, "AI as an Image Generator for Comic Books and Graphic Novels," is a low-stakes way for you (and your students) to ease into using AI because it isn't coaching them on the writing; instead, AI offers images to compliment the memoirs they've already written. We are especially excited about how AI can act as an artist to enhance a writer's work. It will be powerful, if you use this lesson, to talk about the implications of using AI in this way.

It's possible that students want to keep their memoirs as they are. If students are keeping their memoirs as beautiful pieces of prose (or verse), we suggest that they create class anthologies, like we introduce in Lesson 6. Sorting pieces into anthologies leads to powerful conversations about underlying themes, characterization, and ways to categorize stories.

Another way to turn ownership over to students is when it comes to celebration. Do they have a particular way they'd like to celebrate their work? Should they host a schoolwide or community-based event? If so, how should it run? We find, as with most other parts of the writing process, kids will take ownership when they have choice. You can read more about ways to celebrate in the conclusion of the book.

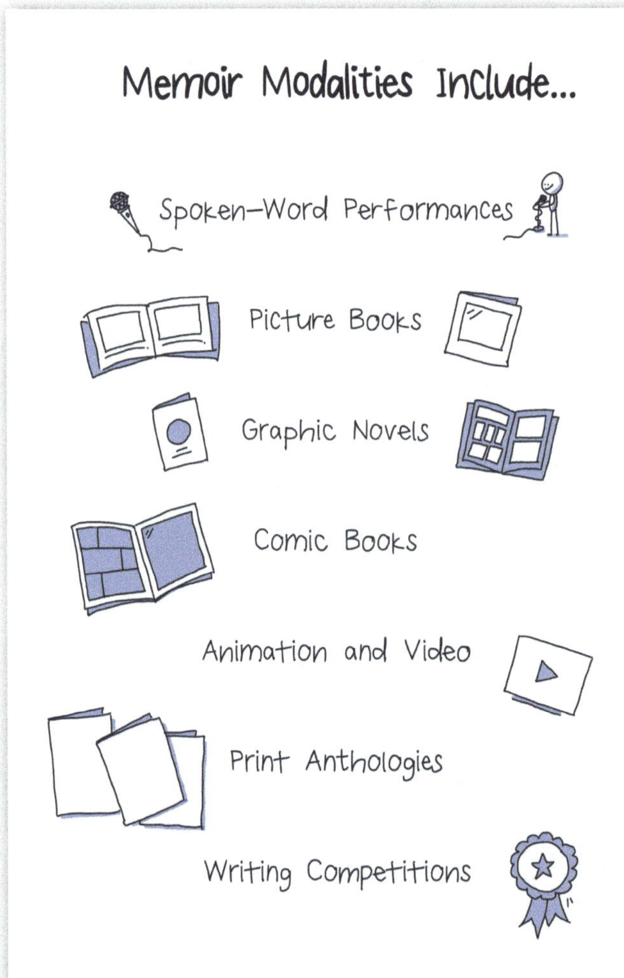

Lesson 1

Exploring Memoir Modalities—Immersion in Mentors

STRATEGY

Contemporary writers know that they can publish their writing in a variety of modalities, from spoken-word performances, to illustrated books, to animated videos, to writing competitions. To figure out what modality suits them, writers immerse themselves in mentor texts, investigating which modalities might enhance their work.

Visit hs-guidetoteaching.org to access a collection of mentors in multiple modalities.

USE THIS STRATEGY...to get your writers excited to publish and to explore ways that memoir exists in the world that your writers can be part of.

Inquiry Question

How do memoirists publish, and which of these modalities am I drawn to?

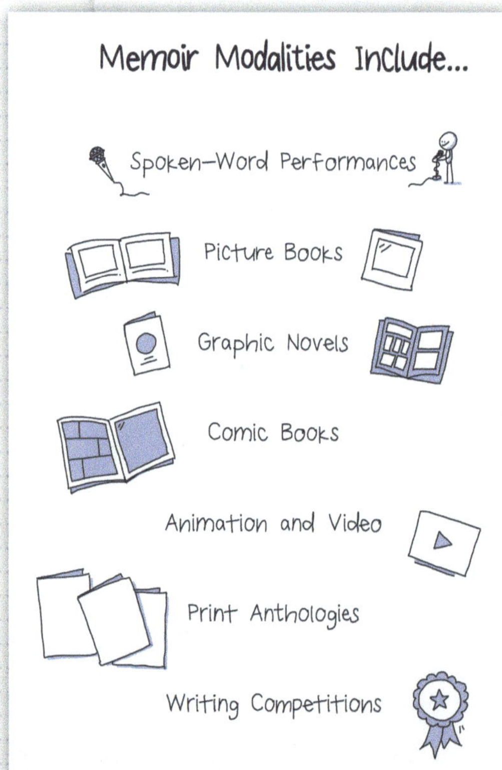

LAUNCH THE INQUIRY

- Suggest to your students that writers publish their memoirs in a variety of modalities, and the best way for them to choose which modality suits them, and their draft, best is to explore mentor texts.
- Show a chart of memoir modalities, and demonstrate how you might choose a modality that would match and enhance your memoir.
- Share a collection of mentors, and give students time to explore several and to talk with a partner about what they are drawn to.
- Invite students to end by planning the work entailed in publishing their piece; clarify deadlines, and if helpful, set up teams.

When Mary demonstrated, she talked with students about how her story felt very intimate, and she wasn't sure about doing a spoken-word performance, so maybe she would seek other writers who wanted to publish in print, as an anthology of collected memoirs.

Lauren, on the other hand, when she demonstrated, was drawn to Kobe Bryant's *Dear Basketball* (2020), with its animated movie that plays behind the narration. She talked about exploring iMovie or other software to create a video.

Coley thought about using photographs and other images to turn her memoir into a scrapbook or photo essay. She weighed whether to do this on Canva, digitally, or to do it by hand.

PROMPTS TO COACH STUDENTS AND PARTNERSHIPS

If you love to draw, or love media, you might enhance your memoir by developing it with these media.

Don't feel you need to be an expert at art or media. AI can help you illustrate. You can essentially be the designer, while your AI partner acts as your artist.

This is a great moment for collaboration. Your partner might be a beautiful water colorist, or great with iMovie, and you can partner up to harness these powers.

CLASSROOM ARTIFACTS

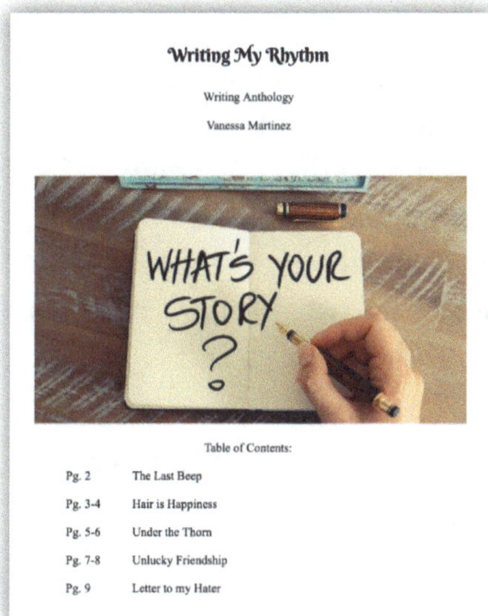

Writing My Rhythm

Writing Anthology

Vanessa Martinez

Table of Contents:

Writers publish in different modalities.

Lesson 2

Using the Expertise of All Students to Publish

STRATEGY

Writers learn to meet deadlines, and when possible, they help each other to meet these deadlines by harnessing their collective strengths.

Visit hs-guidetoteaching.org to access a chart on ways writers can support each other.

USE THIS STRATEGY...to coach students in creating work plans, paying attention to a calendar with dates and deadlines, and turning to each other for support with tasks. This lesson can also help students focus on supporting each other, while you also give them more work time overall.

Ways to Actively Support Fellow Writers While Preparing for Publication

Make work plans with deadlines in mind	Read a writer's piece and give precise feedback as a reader
Review AI suggestions	Encourage each other to submit to journals & competitions
Listen to a writer and transcribe–sections or a whole text	Share digital skills, especially with media
Share art and illustration skills	Organize pieces to publish anthologies
Remind each other of deadlines and tasks	Ask who needs help, offer to help
Create invitations to events	Create online sites to host pieces
Rehearse for oral presentations	Let others know about events and publishings

TEACH THE STRATEGY

- Suggest to students that all writers, and everyone who works on publishing projects, learn to support each other as deadlines approach.
- Invite students to share ideas for ways they could be helpful to each other.
- Share a chart of Ways to Actively Support Fellow Writers. (You can make your own with students or share this one.)
- Invite students to share with a partner what they might be able to do to be helpful, and have them share any skills that might help others in the class. (Some might offer seminars, for example, on iMovie, Image Generation, Canva, or other media.)
- Give students work time to focus on creating work plans and getting started with the publishing process.

PROMPTS TO COACH STUDENTS AND PARTNERSHIPS

It often helps to create a list of tasks that you need to complete, and a calendar with your deadline on it, and then move some of these tasks onto your calendar, thinking of other commitments you have as well.

Sometimes a task that would be really daunting for one writer is easy for another, and vice versa, because we have different skill sets. Ask for help. Offer help.

Some publishing projects need to be collaborative, like organizing anthologies. Organize a team or assign an editor to take on some of the organizational skills.

CLASSROOM ARTIFACTS

Students created a flyer for the community event.

Learning Session	Sign Up
• Using iMovie to make a Digital Memoir, Hosted by: Chloè	• Cayla • Elijah • Jayme
• Graphic Novel Techniques, Hosted by: Noah	• Pooja • Isa • Blair
• Using the Podcasting Software, Hosted by: Leo	• Matteo • Roman • Cole • Hope

A sample sign-up sheet for student-led seminars.

Lesson 3

Matching Register to Audience

STRATEGY

Writers consider their audience, matching their overall register (tone, word choice, linguistic choices) to the audience, thinking about the age, experience, and expectations of their intended audience.

USE THIS STRATEGY...to give students choice over their language and content, while teaching them some wise ways to think about those choices.

- You'll find a lesson on linguistic choices and register in Chapter 3, Lesson 7.

Visit hs-guidetoteaching.org to access the teaching chart and a collection of mentor memoirs that are particularly matched to specific audiences.

TEACH THE STRATEGY

To reach specific audiences, writers consider...

- difficulty/complexity
- word choice
- explicit violence
- implicit violence
- other mature content
- register
- audience knowledge
- audience passion

- Ask students to talk with a partner about why movies in the United States tend to have ratings, like PG, R, and X.
- Summarize how these ratings let audiences know what to expect. Suggest that, similarly, stories tend to be divided into children's literature, young adult literature, and novels for adults.
- Invite students to talk in partnerships about what content might shape these decisions about the intended audience for a narrative. Create an informal chart.
- Watch snippets of some spoken-word performances, inviting students to compare the intended/appropriate audience for each and the authors' decisions. (We suggest Alfonso Lacayo's "Bad Haircut," Emi Mahmoud's "Individual World Poetry Slam Finals 2015," and Kobe Bryant's "Dear Basketball." All available on YouTube or linked on our website.)

When Lauren worked with her class, students talked about how sometimes the audience might be less about age than about what groups love, like basketball. They noted Emi Mahmoud's narrative of violence and use of mature language, as compared to Alfonso Lacayo's humor and self-deprecation. Lauren's students decided that they would show "Bad Haircut" to middle school students, and Emi Mahmoud's performance to high school students and adults.

- End by suggesting your writers talk with a partner about their specific, intended audience, and what revision suggestions that decision might suggest. Then give them work time to prepare to publish.

PROMPTS TO COACH STUDENTS AND PARTNERSHIPS

You can label your work specifically for an audience just as film-makers do—like you could make your anthology a YA anthology.

Picture books are especially interesting, especially those written for older readers.

If you are adding images, think about the content of these images and your intended audience, and you can make thoughtful decisions about what those images look like.

CLASSROOM ARTIFACTS

Intended Audience: Middle and high school students

Justification: This is meant for middle and high school students because of the language and content. Sharing how my brother talks about me and my feelings feels mature.

This writer reflects on their content as well as language and marks their text as written for middle and high school readers.

Lesson 4

Picture Book Illustrations Play Several Roles

STRATEGY

Picture book authors know that the illustrations can play a wide range of roles, from simply evoking mood to enhancing narrative elements. Novice picture book authors often study published books to investigate the variety of roles that illustrations play in these books.

Visit hs-guidetoteaching.org to access a collection of picture book memoirs that have particularly compelling and significant illustrations.

USE THIS STRATEGY...for your memoir writers who are interested in turning their writing into picture books, so they can see the wide range of functions illustrations can have.

> **Inquiry Question**
>
> What roles can illustrations play in picture book memoirs, and which of these roles might I try with my illustrations?

LAUNCH THE INQUIRY

- Suggest to your writers that picture book authors have an extra tool because their illustrations add meaning in the book. You might reference Jacqueline Woodson's process. Woodson describes how she revises her written narrative based on the illustrations, and how the illustrations give extra secrets in the text (2025).
- Share a small collection of picture book memoirs, and invite students to investigate the role that illustrations play in these books. You might study one page together first, to launch their investigations.

When Coley did this with work with her class, she studied this page from *Watercress*, written by Andrea Wang and illustrated by Jason Chin (2021). Chin's illustrations deepen the theme of a longing for assimilation that runs through this narrative, through poignant symbolism and a color palette that captures a sense of old American cars, a Midwestern landscape, and a family that stands out.

- Create a quick chart of student insights to support their ongoing work.
- Invite authors to work collaboratively or alone, with art supplies (watercolors, colored pencils, crayons, etc.) or with AI to draft illustrations for their picture books.

PROMPTS TO COACH STUDENTS AND PARTNERSHIPS

Working by hand can be really beautiful, even if you're uncertain about your artistic skills. You might try watercolor washes, which can create simple abstracts to evoke parts of your text.

Sometimes you might want to find a photo from a family collection, or old photos from your phone, that can anchor your piece.

You can work with an AI partner, training it to create images that you like. It helps if you have mentor texts for it, and you need to be willing to go through multiple rounds of revision.

CLASSROOM ARTIFACTS

I am writing a memoir about a track race, my senior year in high school. I've uploaded it here. I'd like you to create an image of a track that is set up for hurdles. I'd like it to not have any people on it, but I want the race course to look lonely and intimidating. Please try an image, using muted colors, in a kind of watercolor and ink style.

Mary tried creating art to go with her memoir drawing by hand and using AI.

Prepping for Spoken-Word Events

Lesson 5

STRATEGY

Students opting for spoken word often study spoken-word performers they admire to learn presentation techniques. Then they practice their presentations again and again, trying out and adapting these techniques to enhance their own pieces.

USE THIS STRATEGY... to inspire students to bring their whole bodies to their presentations and to continually turn to mentors across the writing process. Often, students will also be inspired to speak without a script, which takes extra preparation.

Visit hs-guidetoteaching.org to access a collection of spoken-word performances and teaching charts to support preparing for these performances.

Inquiry Question

What techniques do spoken word performers use to enhance their presentations, and which of these techniques do I want to practice to enhance mine?

LAUNCH THE INQUIRY

- Suggest to students that spoken-word performers take the performance aspect of their piece seriously, and they lean on specific techniques for spoken-word performances and speeches.
- Invite students to study one spoken-word performer with you to investigate the techniques their performance suggests.
- With your students, generate a chart of spoken-word performance techniques.
- Share a collection of mentors, and invite students to study these in partnerships, investigating how these other performers use these (and other) techniques.
- Suggest that students begin practicing their performances, trying out these presentation techniques as they do so.

Spoken-Word Performance Techniques

- deliberate eye contact
- speaking without a script (memorized)
- guestures that show what's happening
- changes in tone of voice
- shifts in tone
- shifts in pacing (faster vs. slower)
- taking on voices of characters
- deliberate pauses
- directly addressing the audience
- emoting-expressing story emotions

When Lauren did this work with her class, she returned to Alfonso Lacayo's "Bad Haircut" from *The Moth* (2015), and generated a chart like the one above.

Lesson 5
(Continued)

PROMPTS TO COACH STUDENTS AND PARTNERSHIPS

One of the hardest tasks is memorization, and you want to start that right away. Remember, it doesn't have to be word for word; it just has to capture the feeling of each part.

It can be helpful to record yourself and play it back, looking for places you want to tuck in other details, pause, or make adjustments. You could also try this with a partner and have them offer you some tips.

Studying presentations like TED Talks can also be helpful. Look for moves the speakers make that you want to emulate, then practice them.

CLASSROOM ARTIFACTS

Tips for Performing Your Memoir (Without a Script!)

How actors, poets, and speakers get ready to memorize and perform

1. Break It Into Chunks

Instead of memorizing the whole thing at once, divide your piece into smaller sections (like scenes or paragraphs).

Practice one chunk until it flows. Then add the next. Always go back to the beginning.

✓ This helps you remember the order and builds confidence!

2. Move Your Body

Use natural movements or gestures while practicing.

Walk a few steps, gesture with your hands, look around—tie your words to motion.

Your brain remembers better when your body gets involved.

3. Listen to Yourself

Record yourself reading your piece, then listen to it a few times (while walking, doing chores, relaxing).

Try repeating parts out loud without looking.

Hearing your voice helps lock in the rhythm and flow.

4. Feel What You're Saying

Don't just "say the words"—feel them. Spoken word is about emotion and truth.

If you connect to the meaning, the words are easier to remember.

People will feel it with you, and that's what makes it powerful.

Final Tip: It's okay if it's not word-for-word!

Spoken word is real and raw. If you forget a line, keep going with the heart of your story.

What matters most is your voice, your truth, and your presence.

Help students memorize and perform their pieces with specific tips.

Sifting Memoirs into Anthologies

Lesson 6

STRATEGY

Editors know that there are multiple ways to sort memoirs into anthologies. They read stories, then ask: What are possible categories this story fits into? Then they gather their stories together, matching them to different anthologies.

USE THIS STRATEGY...to support your writers who want to publish their pieces in an anthology, showing them how to act as editors, helping them think about different categories stories can fall into.

Visit hs-guidetoteaching.org to access some favorite YA memoir anthologies.

TEACH THE STRATEGY

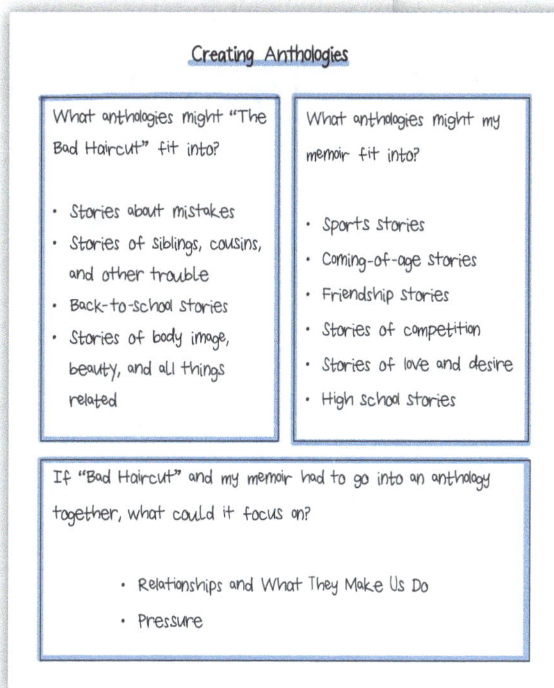
Creating Anthologies

What anthologies might "The Bad Haircut" fit into?

- Stories about mistakes
- Stories of siblings, cousins, and other trouble
- Back-to-school stories
- Stories of body image, beauty, and all things related

What anthologies might my memoir fit into?

- Sports stories
- Coming-of-age stories
- Friendship stories
- Stories of competition
- Stories of love and desire
- High school stories

If "Bad Haircut" and my memoir had to go into an anthology together, what could it focus on?

- Relationships and What They Make Us Do
- Pressure

- Suggest to your writers that anthologies are usually organized around some kind of category that the stories included fit into. If you have some YA memoir anthologies, show them (e.g., *Come on In*, *We Ae Displaced, #NotYourPrincess*).
- Take a familiar story that your students know, and invite students to think how it might fit into several possible categories/anthologies. You can return to your demonstration writing or a published memoir.
- Study a second memoir, this time asking:
  - Could this memoir fit into the same anthology as the first?
  - Do we need a new anthology?
  - Could we invent a new category that would fit both?

When Mary did this with her class, first, they analyzed what categories "Bad Haircut" might fit into. Then, they revisited her track memoir and brainstormed categories into which her memoir might fit. After that, she and her students thought about categories that might fit if the memoirs were to go in an anthology together.

Depending on how many students are publishing in anthologies, you can have very loose categories, like "High School Stories," or "Family Stories," or narrower ones, like "Cruel Friends."

- Set up students to review the memoirs that will be published in anthologies and to suggest a few possible anthologies that will house these memoirs.
- When ready, students can begin to order pieces and work on a table of contents for these anthologies and author bios.

PROMPTS TO COACH STUDENTS AND PARTNERSHIPS

It helps to read each other's stories as if they are fiction stories, asking "What is this about?" and "What else is this about?"

Sometimes an anthology can be organized by topic, or by kind of character, or by theme, or by age group. You could have some shorter anthologies and some longer ones.

It's helpful to also think about what else goes in an anthology, such as a table of contents and an author bio.

CLASSROOM ARTIFACTS

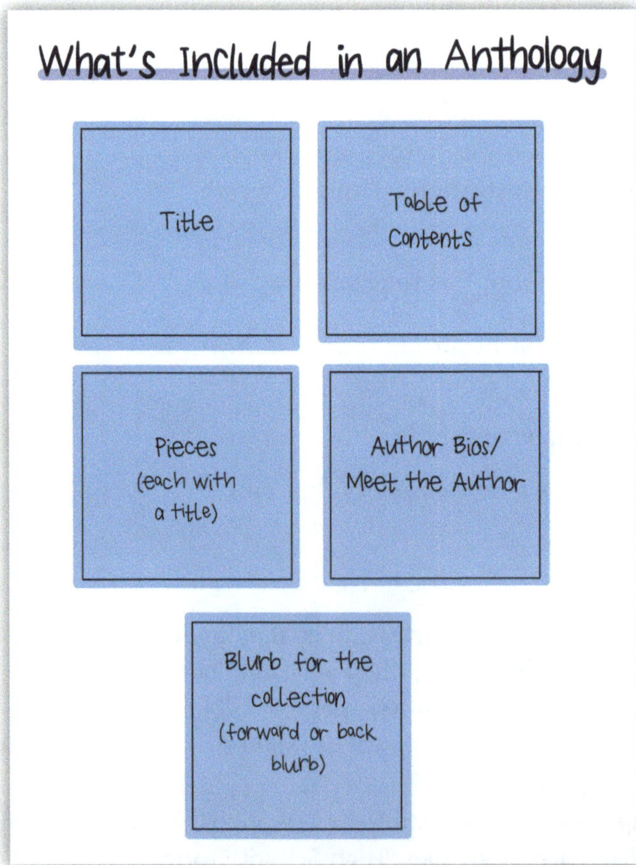

Chart to help writers organize and arrange a classroom anthology.

AI as an Image Generator for Comic Books and Graphic Novels

Lesson 7

STRATEGY

Writers know that they can create their own illustrations or they can seek help from an AI image generator. When turning to an AI image generator, two strategies are especially helpful: giving very specific instructions and being willing to revise multiple times.

USE THIS STRATEGY... to support writers who are uneasy about creating their own illustrations but would like to publish in a graphic novel or comic book format.

Visit hs-guidetoteaching.org to access the teaching chart.

TEACH THE STRATEGY

- Suggest to your writers who want to publish in comic book/manga/graphic novel format that they can draw their own images, or they can turn to an AI image generator as a partner. Lead students to an AI partner for image generation your school allows, such as MagicSchool AI, Adobe Firefly, Perplexity, DALL-E 3, or Canva.
- Explain how you prompt an AI image generation partner. Invite students who are experienced to share tips. Cocreate or share a chart.
- Demonstrate prompting AI with your own memoir, using some of the tips sourced by the class.
- Coach students interested in this work to build their initial AI prompts, reminding them to go scene by scene and expect to revise.

When prompting an AI image generator, it's helpful to...

- describe the genre you are writing.
- upload a page from a mentor text.
- give details of the scene to illustrate:
    - be specific with characters & emotions.
    - describe the setting in detail.
    - mention clothing, props or symbols.
- make suggestions about mood & tone.
- say "graphic novel style" or style of an artist.
- give feedback on results; ask for revision.
- reference your AI partner in endnotes, footnotes, or acknolwedgements - and mentor artists too!

PROMPTS TO COACH STUDENTS AND PARTNERSHIPS

Remember to acknowledge your AI partner, in a footnote or endnote or acknowledgment. If you mirrored an artist's style, acknowledge that artist as well.

AI works best with smaller chunks of text. You could feed it each scene of your story and ask for images or comics. Think about what to ask AI for, so you can add to the story, by tucking in extra action, details, or secrets.

Try out multiple styles and drafts. You can ask AI for revisions by saying things like "Try this in color" or "Make this feel spookier to match my mood." Tinkering with what it offers you is part of the fun!

CLASSROOM ARTIFACTS

Please generate an illustration, in graphic novel style. The illustration should show this part of my memoir. Ideally, I'd like this graphic novel not to be people-focused, so maybe try other images. Here's an excerpt from my memoir: There's something about a ritual that offers a little extra joy. Where routines make life feel monotonous, rituals give life meaning. They bring us back to the present, rooting us in the moment.

When I think of the rituals that my family holds onto, none come to mind– we're not religious, we don't care for holidays, we don't vacation in the same place every year. Seeing my friends have these constants, I wondered whether or not we should create these? I knew my family would laugh at the suggestion. Maybe it's just not who we are...

Then I remembered the beach.

I really like the style you created here. Could we try it another way? Maybe this time with a better representation around the lack of religion, holidays, and vacations in my family.

Coley prompted her AI partner to create an illustration in graphic novel style, then she gave her AI partner some feedback.

Conclusion: Publishing, Reflection, and Assessment

A memoir is an invitation into another person's privacy.
—*Isabel Allende*

Isabel Allende speaks of memoir as a breach of privacy. Memoir writing takes courage, humor, and self-analysis. The memoir writer opens up some part of their life and lays it bare for themselves and their peers. It may be this revelatory, risky nature of memoir that makes it so compelling to read. Audiences love memoir, especially short memoirs like the ones your students will produce.

Next, you'll find some suggestions for publishing, reflection, and assessment. Linger for a moment before wrapping this work up. Hearing each other's stories is one way to develop sympathetic imaginations, to briefly see the world through someone else's eyes. Surely this world needs more of that.

Publishing

As you think about publishing, think about how to have your students' words reach real audiences.

You might gather students' anthologies, picture books, and graphic novels, and see if your local coffee shop or public library will display them. You can be sure that families and friends will find their way to these spaces to read. You might ask that same space if you can have an authors' night, inviting families to browse informally and talk to authors, or to hear a few read out loud.

If your students have created spoken-word performances, we encourage you to host a *Moth*-style or *StoryCorp*-style event, where students perform their pieces for family and friends, perhaps in different classrooms along a hall or at the library. If they've created videos, have a video premiere.

Some of your students might submit their pieces to the *Scholastic Art & Writing Awards*, or to teen writing journals such as *Teen Ink*, *Polyphony Lit*, or *Stone Soup*.

The main thing is that something needs to happen with students' writing, so they participate fully in the arc of the writing process, which includes response from an audience. When young writers see their writing existing in the world, when their words visibly reach into their community, they are inspired to work at their writing.

Reflection

The act of writing memoir is itself reflection, but it's also worth it to invite your writers to reflect on what they learned about each other and themselves, as writers and as people.

Regardless of the bigger, classwide celebration, you might invite students to publish in small writing groups (combine partnerships), and to share with each other what they were impressed by, what stuck with them about each other's pieces and each other's experiences. Some students benefit from simple sentence starters or cue cards, as the art of complimenting each other on their work is still new to them.

Compliment Cards

I love the way you...	It reminded me of...	It made me think about...
I didn't realize before...	One part/line I loved was...	It made me feel...

You'll also want to invite your students to reflect on what they're proud of, and how they've grown as writers. Taking a moment now to reflect on skills and habits they've developed will make it more likely your students will deploy these skills and habits in fresh situations.

Some students will also benefit from simple sentence starters or cue cards to help them reflect on themselves as writers. Partners can "play a card," and the other partner can talk off of it, as one way to help writers launch these conversations, or they can freewrite from these cards.

Reflection Cards

I'm proud of...	One thing I found challenging was...	An author I came to know better is...
I worked hard at...	I'm better at...	Next time, I'll...

Take a moment to use these same cards to reflect on your teaching. Too often, we celebrate the kids as writers but don't take time to celebrate ourselves as teachers. Grab your colleagues, and tell each other what you're proud of. Write a quick note to a parent about a particular kid, or to all your students' parents. Let your principal know how proud you are of the kids so they'll be proud of you. Tell your partner, your dog, your cat, your spider plant.

Assessment

We think about assessment and grading as slightly different things, with grading being one part of and one way to assess. Assessment is something you are doing every day, every time you talk with a kid about their writing, or listen to their partnership conversation, or skim their EdTech chats, or study their drafts. As a teacher, assessment is akin to breathing. You're learning about your kids, making judgments, adjusting your instruction all the time, and you don't pause to document it all.

Grading is different. All secondary teachers know that grading is the bête noire that haunts us. It is the thing that leaves us feeling uneasy, unsure about the precise fairness of our grades, absolutely sure that we take too long to give grades, and quietly worried about the effect (and lack of effect) of the grades we give students. We've spent a lot of time studying assessment and grading. We share some of that thinking here.

Grading

For a deep discussion of grading, including ways to reform grading practices so that they support student achievement (and do the least harm possible), we suggest starting with Joe Feldman's *Grading for Equity* (2024), a powerful and thought-provoking text. A great text to pair with it is *Making Thinking Visible* (2011), by Ritchhart et al. and *Collective Student Efficacy* (2021), by Hattie et al. Two watershed (and very short) texts to consider are Doug Reeve's (2004) "The Case Against the Zero," and Howard Johnston's (2011) "Best Practices in Grading." We also love Guskey et al.'s (2024) *Grading with Integrity,* and Guskey's (2006) article, "Making High School Grades Meaningful." Visit hs-guidetoteaching.org to access a list of texts you might consider for a study group on grading.

What all of these scholars agree on is that grading has the potential to do harm to students—to limit their motivation to write, to damage their confidence as writers, or to create writers whose only motivation is a letter or a number. Feldman looks closely at how grading affects motivation, and he encourages teachers to think about practices that will inform students and families of their progress toward important benchmarks, rather than their compliance within sometimes very old systems. Reeves reminds us that a very low score, especially when schools use numerical systems of 0–100, can make it impossible for students to recuperate and don't offer students any way to grow and change. It's all worth reading, and we encourage you to do your best as an individual to grade ethically and in a way that doesn't harm young people, and to form committees to read and research contemporary practices in grading.

We also know that you work within a system that you may have little control over or voice within. We offer a few tools that may be helpful as you navigate assessment, self-assessment, and grading. These include checklists, which are most helpful for kids, and rubrics, which are necessary for teachers.

A note about rubrics: we did a lot of studying of rubrics, particularly with Ray Pecheone, executive director of SCALE (Stanford Center for Assessment, Learning, and Equity) at Stanford. We developed a few characteristics of effective student-facing rubrics in our collaboration, that we share here.

Characteristics of Student-Facing Rubrics	
Accessible language	Rubrics are most often useful for the people who wrote them, usually because their language is so arcane. To make rubrics useful to students, use language that bridges social and academic language.
Formative "how-to" steps to advance levels	A lot of rubrics (IB, AP, SAT) are *summative*, which means they are useful only for scoring. Students need *formative* rubrics, ones that include practical steps they can follow to raise the level of their work (usually from left to right).
Asset-based criteria	Avoid all deficit language, such as "did not" or "only." A student's first step should be to get on the rubric, and that's a positive step. Then they can look at the next criterion and say "If I do that, I can move up,"' and it should be a positive step.
Include only the benchmarks that are an option	Don't include the "well below benchmark" as an option. Start your rubric with an accessible starting point, so that students can enter the rubric, and focus on the levels students should work within and strive for.
Allow for interstices	Instead of wordsmithing the spaces between levels, leave those as blanks, as there are a lot of ways writing may grow and change, and that leaves you and your students room for flexibility (e.g., the score of 3.5).

Feedback

It's important to distinguish between grading and feedback. John Hattie's (2023) review of over 2,100 meta-analyses show how significant feedback can be to accelerating achievement—feedback that is given in the moment, is calibrated, and is followed by the immediate opportunity for repeated practice (Frey et al. 2018). Good feedback helps students cultivate awareness of their decision-making within the learning processes and the steps they can take to revise their work and move it forward (Frey et al. 2018). Feedback is what you give your students every time you talk to them about their writing while they are writing. It is what a peer partner and an AI partner can give, across the writing process. Overall, we try to maximize the time and effort we put into feedback and to make our grading as concise and civilized as possible.

It's also important to conceive of student work *as* feedback. "First and foremost, teachers have to see student work and performance as feedback to themselves" (Frey et al., 2018). As you study student work across the writing process, think about it as feedback for how students are responding to instruction, to curriculum.

Self-Assessment

We do believe in self-assessment and in collective assessment. It's tremendously helpful for students to self-assess their writing and their writing process, so they can note how they are growing, and set goals for themselves for their next writing project. Frey et al. (2018) remind us it's important for students to develop an internal compass that drives independent learning, rather than being dependent on a teacher to determine next steps. Tools are helpful in this process—checklists and rubrics. We've provided samples of each of these. In general, checklists are most helpful for kids, as they reflect on what they've done and set goals for next steps.

We learned a few things from Ray Pecheone (2015) that transformed the effectiveness of our checklists. They include:

- Write the checklist in an "I" voice—it makes it more personal.
- Include checkboxes. Checking off a list is satisfying.
- Include practical, "how-to" steps for how to reach criteria.
- Pair checklists with annotated exemplars.
- Teach students to practice self-assessment and annotation with a partner.

A Writer's Checklist for Memoir

Meaning

- ☐ I chose a moment or event to explore that is suggestive of deeper issues or themes or that reveals aspects of relationships.
- ☐ I developed meaning through describing personal experiences and reflection.

Structure

- ☐ I structured my piece deliberately, perhaps to:
  - ☐ develop the narrative.
  - ☐ enhance meaning.
  - ☐ delay full understanding.
- ☐ I led my reader considerately from one part to the next, using transitional phrases or cues so that the reader can follow:
  - ☐ shifts in time.
  - ☐ shifts in perspective.

Craft

- ☐ I oriented my reader at the start of my piece, sharing essential information about:
  - ☐ who is in the story.
  - ☐ where and when the story takes place.
  - ☐ underlying issues (or hints of these).
  - ☐ my voice and perspective as the narrator.
- ☐ I developed tension, perhaps by:
  - ☐ foreshadowing.
  - ☐ careful pacing.
- ☐ I used narrative techniques to make the story engaging, such as:
  - ☐ vivid imagery.
  - ☐ symbolism.
  - ☐ poetic or figurative language.
  - ☐ dialogue.
- ☐ I included inner thinking as a means of sharing feelings and/or insights
- ☐ I provided some resolution or closure at the end, such as:
  - ☐ lessons learned.
  - ☐ insights or epiphanies.
  - ☐ hints of possible change.

Access the full checklist at hs-guidetoteaching.org.

Rubrics theoretically help teachers and kids envision how to raise the level of their writing, but to work this way, rubrics need to be asset-based, with practical "how-to" steps, so that first, they get on the rubric (a good thing), then they can see how to work their way up levels. Overall, we focus on formative rubrics—ones that will help students improve. We may, eventually, find ourselves needing to use a summative rubric such as an IB or AP rubric, but we know that along the way, students need more supportive tools. AI can partner with you in creating asset-based, formative rubrics that include practical steps for writers to raise the level of their work.

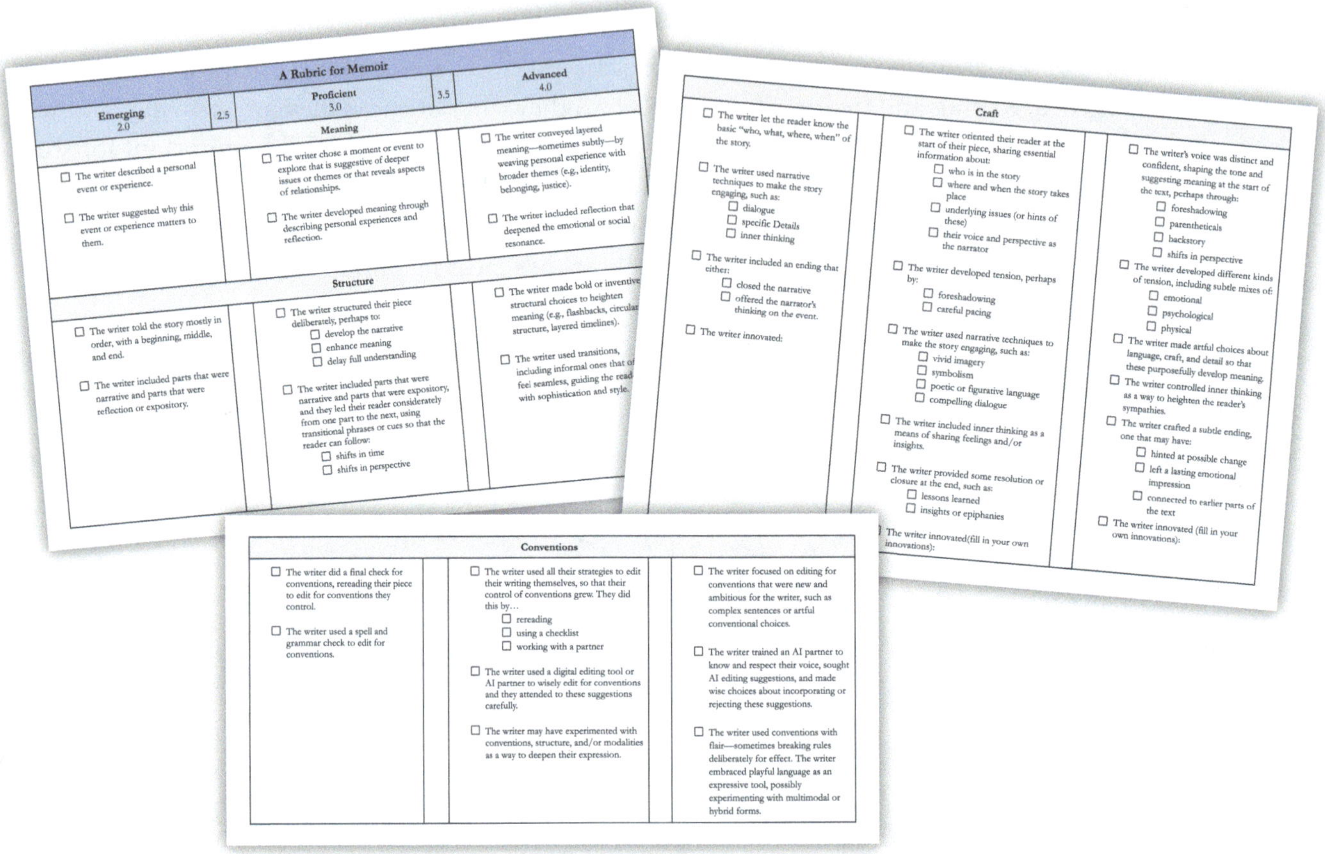

A Rubric for Memoir

Emerging 2.0	2.5	Proficient 3.0	3.5	Advanced 4.0
Meaning				
☐ The writer described a personal event or experience. ☐ The writer suggested why this event or experience matters to them.		☐ The writer chose a moment or event to explore that is suggestive of deeper issues or themes or that reveals aspects of relationships. ☐ The writer developed meaning through describing personal experiences and reflection.		☐ The writer conveyed layered meaning—sometimes subtly—by weaving personal experience with broader themes (e.g., identity, belonging, justice). ☐ The writer included reflection that deepened the emotional or social resonance.
Structure				
☐ The writer told the story mostly in order, with a beginning, middle, and end. ☐ The writer included parts that were narrative and parts that were reflection or expository.		☐ The writer structured their piece deliberately, perhaps to: ☐ develop the narrative ☐ enhance meaning ☐ delay full understanding ☐ The writer included parts that were narrative and parts that were expository, and they led their reader considerately from one part to the next, using transitional phrases or cues so that the reader can follow: ☐ shifts in time ☐ shifts in perspective		☐ The writer made bold or inventive structural choices to heighten meaning (e.g., flashbacks, circular structure, layered timelines). ☐ The writer used transitions, including informal ones that of feel seamless, guiding the read with sophistication and style.

Craft				
☐ The writer let the reader know the basic "who, what, where, when" of the story. ☐ The writer used narrative techniques to make the story engaging, such as: ☐ dialogue ☐ specific Details ☐ inner thinking ☐ The writer included an ending that either: ☐ closed the narrative ☐ offered the narrator's thinking on the event. ☐ The writer innovated:		☐ The writer oriented their reader at the start of their piece, sharing essential information about: ☐ who is in the story ☐ where and when the story takes place ☐ underlying issues (or hints of these) ☐ their voice and perspective as the narrator ☐ The writer developed tension, perhaps by: ☐ foreshadowing ☐ careful pacing ☐ The writer used narrative techniques to make the story engaging, such as: ☐ vivid imagery ☐ symbolism ☐ poetic or figurative language ☐ compelling dialogue ☐ The writer included inner thinking as a means of sharing feelings and/or insights. ☐ The writer provided some resolution or closure at the end, such as: ☐ lessons learned ☐ insights or epiphanies ☐ The writer innovated(fill in your own innovations):		☐ The writer's voice was distinct and confident, shaping the tone and suggesting meaning at the start of the text, perhaps through: ☐ foreshadowing ☐ parentheticals ☐ backstory ☐ shifts in perspective ☐ The writer developed different kinds of tension, including subtle mixes of: ☐ emotional ☐ psychological ☐ physical ☐ The writer made artful choices about language, craft, and detail so that these purposefully develop meaning. ☐ The writer controlled inner thinking as a way to heighten the reader's sympathies. ☐ The writer crafted a subtle ending, one that may have: ☐ hinted at possible change ☐ left a lasting emotional impression ☐ connected to earlier parts of the text ☐ The writer innovated (fill in your own innovations):

Conventions				
☐ The writer did a final check for conventions, rereading their piece to edit for conventions they control. ☐ The writer used a spell and grammar check to edit for conventions.		☐ The writer used all their strategies to edit their writing themselves, so that their control of conventions grew. They did this by… ☐ rereading ☐ using a checklist ☐ working with a partner ☐ The writer used a digital editing tool or AI partner to wisely edit for conventions and they attended to these suggestions carefully. ☐ The writer may have experimented with conventions, structure, and/or modalities as a way to deepen their expression.		☐ The writer focused on editing for conventions that were new and ambitious for the writer, such as complex sentences or artful conventional choices. ☐ The writer trained an AI partner to know and respect their voice, sought AI editing suggestions, and made wise choices about incorporating or rejecting these suggestions. ☐ The writer used conventions with flair—sometimes breaking rules deliberately for effect. The writer embraced playful language as an expressive tool, possibly experimenting with multimodal or hybrid forms.

Celebrating and Planning for Next Time

Teaching is a maelstrom. By the time you pick up these lessons to teach the unit again, you'll have vague recollections of what you loved and what you'd change—how lovely if you also have a few detailed notes, and maybe a couple of favorite student pieces as exemplars.

Make some notes and gather some materials for the next time you teach. Our kids' writing is feedback on our teaching, our curriculum. Were there some lessons that you could combine as micro lessons, because the kids picked them up quickly? Could you relegate some to teach only to your outliers—your most proficient or most novice writers? Did you need more or less time at any point? Was there any moment when students weren't writing enough? Did you wish you had previewed something earlier?

Mostly, though, linger in the deeper relationships you have with students, and they have with each other, because you did this work. In *Reader, Come Home*, (2018), brain researcher Maryanne Wolf describes how you can track two parts of the brain that grow when someone becomes a reader. One is the part of the brain responsible for analytic thinking. The other is the part responsible for empathy. When we read stories, we literally become more empathetic. With this work, you incited the young people in your care to write their own and read each other's stories. You've helped make your community just that little bit more empathetic.

Appendices
Sample Memoirs

Appendix A: Mary's Memoir

Just Before the Race

Lisa and I were stretching by the starting line, talking about the race. It was Nationals. The 1/4 - mile hurdles. A national title. A college scholarship.

"I wish we could both win," I said.

Lisa stretched her leg behind her and barely glanced up. "It doesn't work like that, Mary."

Just then Chris came by. Chris, whom I adored. Chris, the fastest boy in New York State. He put his hand on my neck, under my hair. "I hope you win," he whispered, putting his hand on my neck, under my hair, a gossamer touch, the way I loved. "I love how fast you are."

Chris smiled at Lisa. She looked up at him, pulled her long brown hair out of its ponytail, tossed her hair over her shoulders, and stretched one long leg behind her. Chris's eyes widened. When he went up into the stands, Lisa turned and whispered, fiercely, "You're not going to win, you know. Not the race, and not with Chris, either."

Suddenly we saw Mr. Worth, Lisa's dad. Lisa's mom had died two months before, from breast cancer. She had found a lump over a year ago, but her doctor had told her, "It was nothing to worry about." But it was. Since her mom died, Lisa lived alone with her dad, and she was different. She came to school sometimes with bruises on her arms, that she wouldn't talk about. Mr. Worth was strong. He walked toward us, in a dark T-shirt and jeans, the muscles in his arms bulging. Then he stood, right in front of Lisa, close.

"Listen, Lisa, you better win," he said. His voice was hard and low. "Second place is for losers. And there's no room in this family for losers." He clenched his fist. Lisa paled.

The warning gun for the start went off.

To Win or Not to Win...

There were only 100 yards left. Probably 12 seconds. Two more hurdles. My heart beat rapidly, my legs felt like water, but I kept running, harder than I had ever run before, faster. I turned my head for just a moment and listened. I was ahead. I was ahead of Lisa. I could just see her, almost a yard behind. I was going to win. The race. The scholarship. Chris.

Then two things happened, almost at once.

Chris waved from the stands. He stood up. I could hear him cheering my name. I could see his hair gleaming in the sun. He raised his fist, pumping it. I felt as if I could see his eyes, sparkling, laughing, the way they did when he was gloriously happy. His gilded beauty was something glimmering, glorious, galactic.

I quickened my pace even more, ran even harder, even faster. I could feel it would be a record.

One more hurdle. Fifty yards. Probably 6 seconds left. I could hear nothing but my heart, and Lisa's footsteps, right behind me.

Then Mr. Worth stepped out of the shadows by the finish line. He stood, just ahead of us. His face was dark. He raised his fist. It was clenched. I noticed how large his hands were, how his fingers were just the size of the bruises on Lisa's arms. I heard Lisa falter behind me.

I slowed. 3 seconds left.

Even as I ran, I recollected Chris and Lisa, how tangled up together we were. I thought fleetingly about when Chris had arrived on our block. Chris was eight years old and beautiful in a way that would destabilize our neighborhood forever. Lisa made brownies to celebrate his arrival. She gifted me one through the chain link fence that separated our backyards. I put it in my mouth; it was made of mud. I felt soaked with betrayal.

I remembered playing tackle tag in Mrs. Terhaar's yard. How Lisa and I would sprint, evading all others, but decelerating just ahead of Chris. How he would lower us gently to the ground, his arms around our backs. How all I would ever know about desire I learned playing tackle tag in fourth grade, on Mrs. Terhaar's lawn.

Afterward

After the race, Chris came up and put his arm around me. "You did it, Mary," he whispered, pulling my ponytail gently. Then, even lower, "and I know why. I get it."

We both looked over at Lisa, standing next to her dad, who was praising her, his big hands gentle on her back as he hugged her.

My family didn't get it. My coach didn't get it. But Chris did, and Lisa did, and that was enough.

When I think about this race now, it's hard for me to remember anything except confusion and fear. Fear that I didn't understand what was happening in the house next door, fear that I might let my family down by losing and my friend down by winning, and confusion over how this race had come to be about so much more than running fast. I know it felt as if those single seconds were lasting hours, and that no decision I made would make everyone, or maybe anyone, happy.

Ultimately, I put friendship above all else. I regretted it, a little, at the awards dinner, and when my brother was extra kind because I lost. But I was never sorry, really.

Appendix B: Coley's Memoir

Rituals

There's something about a ritual that offers a little extra joy. Where routines make life feel monotonous, rituals give life *meaning*. They bring us back to the present, rooting us in the moment.

When I think of the rituals that my family holds onto, none come to mind–we're not religious, we don't care for holidays, we don't vacation in the same place every year. Seeing my friends have these constants, I wondered whether or not we should create these? I knew my family would laugh at the suggestion. Maybe it's just not who we are...

Then I remembered the beach.

The First Swim

The first swim of the season is an important one–at least for me and my mom. This isn't necessarily the first time we're on the beach for the season. By the time we're ready for the "first swim," we've already taken the walk on the hot sand, put our beach chairs in the spot (a little to the left when you walk on), and put our ankles in the icy water several times.

The first swim is the day when the water is finally warm enough for us to wade in, and, most importantly, dive under the waves. Just like always, the tides have been checked, the Italian subs have been made, the purple cooler has been packed. We walk onto the beach and anchor our matching beach chairs into the sand, hoping this will be the day.

"The waves look pretty good," I say, "I'm feeling good about today."

We sit in our chairs watching the waves pull in and out, looking for a place to enter. In what feels like four seconds later my mom says...

"Let's go. It's time."

Before I can even respond, she's out of her seat, scurrying down to the water. This is how it always goes. She pops up and lets everyone else trail behind her. In typical fashion, I get up quickly to keep pace behind her, only to realize I still have my sunglasses on. I run back to the blanket and toss them down. Take two.

We stand at the edge of the waves, slowly inching our way in. There's a silence between us, a quiet calm. In a world that is constantly pushing us toward dissociation, the ocean has a way of making you feel present–you have no choice but to feel. Back on the sand, I was planning for the future, talking about college and friendships and my brother and our summer plans. Now that we're down here, my mind is still, while my body is pulled out by the tides.

I watch, laughing, as my mom goes under first. While I swan dive in, headfirst, my mom squats and crouches her body in half, fitting under the wave rather than diving into it. She resurfaces, pulling her hair back, the same way as always.

She turns to face me with those beady eyes.

"What?" she asks, "What is it? Are you mocking me out?"

"Just enjoy the water," I quip back.

We weave in and out of the waves for the next hour, sinking into them and letting them carry us up, weightless, before coming back down to earth.

"Alright, what's your score?" I ask.

"8.6, maybe?" my mom says, clearly not settled.

"I know, I get it. We don't want to rank too high too early, but you know sometimes it's only downhill from here." I pause. "I'm going with a solid 9, I think."

This is all part of the routine–we rank the waves. But it's not just the waves. It's the sun, the sand, the water temperature, the crowd level. A 10 is possible, but not easy to achieve. There's a stipulation though: No matter the other factors, you can't rate the day a 10 unless we're together. A beach day with my best friend Lauren can't be a 10, not unless my mom crashed the party, too.

The routine is where we sit, where we enter the water, the purple cooler and the orange blanket.

The ritual is us together, fully present, in the ocean, freed from the future that waits for us on land.

The Last Swim

On a sunny afternoon in mid-September, my mom and I sneak away from the obligations that come with the new fall season to jump in the ocean one more time–until next summer.

By now, the lifeguard chairs have been turned upside down and the beach hut is boarded up; people walk their dogs and sit on benches. We breeze past them, quickly dropping our towels and wading into the warm water. We kept our typical roles, me diving head first into a wave, mom crouching down under one.

"Ah! The saltwater feels so good. And we have this big ocean all to ourselves," I said, flopping back into a wave, sinking down into the water.

"That's local summer," my mom chirped once I floated to the surface.

Local summer is the time of year when all the tourists have migrated back to their homes up north or out west, and the only people left are, well, the locals.

Rituals

The routine will be there next summer–our same spot, the purple cooler, the orange blanket, the Italian subs. The ritual will be there next summer–mom and I, fully present, in the ocean, freed from the future that waits for us on land.

The place that freed us will continue to churn and so will we.

Appendix C: Lauren's Memoir

When the World Goes Silent

I flipped on my blinker and took a breath that didn't feel deep enough. My fingers clutched the steering wheel. It was time to merge onto the highway.

I was driving. I was following my dad—his car steady in front of me, taillights blinking through the rain.

We were on our way to the hospital. The night before, an ambulance took my mom and my littlest brother there. Thinking about it made my stomach clench, so I pushed the thoughts aside.

Right now, I just had to stay in my lane. Merge safely. Follow Dad.

We were going to the hospital. We were going to see them. It would be okay.

Or—I had to believe that it would.

———————

The night before, I had gone to bed early. It was finals, and I was exhausted. I woke up to my mom, sitting on the side of my bed.

"Lauren, wake up," she said, grabbing my shoulders. "You have to come downstairs. Something is wrong with Stephen."

My stomach clenched. We rushed downstairs.

Stephen was on the couch, his body moving in ways that seemed unnatural—jerking, flailing, grinding his teeth. I froze for a moment, like my brain couldn't make sense of what it was seeing. Then, I bolted into action.

"Where's the phone?" I asked.

I picked it up, hands shaking, and dialed 9-1-1. We had practiced in school what to say: our name, the address, the situation. "Hi, this is Lauren Gould," I said, almost breathless. My heart was pounding. "I am at 569 Fern Court. Something is wrong with my brother." My voice caught in my throat. "He is shaking on the couch. His eyes are rolling and he…he's not responding. We need help."

"Stay calm. We'll send an ambulance over to you right now. It should be there in 10-15 minutes," the voice on the other end of the line said.

"They're on the way!" I said to my parents.

The wait for the ambulance was one of the longest 15 minutes of my life. My mom grabbed the phone and called our family friend who was a doctor. "It sounds like he's having a seizure," my mom told us. "All we can do is wait."

One thing they don't show in the movies, is how when you call 9-1-1, and need an ambulance, often the police arrive first. The police, who can't do much, but tell you to keep waiting.

When the police car showed up, sirens blaring and lights flashing, we thought help was here. My dad scooped Stephen up off the couch, and ran outside, carrying him. "My son!" he said. "You need to help my son!"

"You need to wait, sir," the police said back. "We are here to escort the ambulance, but we are not medics."

That night was one of the only times I've ever seen my father cry. Watching the scene unfold, I felt powerless to help. It seemed like Stephen was dying, and there was nothing we could do but wait.

Finally, the ambulance arrived. They put Stephen on a stretcher and loaded him in the back. My mom rode with him. Only one family member was allowed, so my dad took the car and drove behind.

——————

I have two brothers, Austin and Stephen. They are two years apart, and I am much older than them—six and eight years older, respectively. Growing up, I'd always felt more like a second parent than a sibling. I held them when they were babies—fed them bottles and changed their diapers. As they grew, I babysat them. Made them mac 'n' cheese, snuggled them when they were scared, settled their arguments when they fought. They were a pair. We called them AustinandStephen or TheBoys. Always in motion, always fighting, always loud.

With little brothers like that, the joke in my family was: if the house was quiet, something was wrong.

That night, something was wrong.

During the chaos of the wait, Austin had woken up. He had crawled out of bed and come downstairs, and I can only imagine witnessing the same scene I did: our parents, terrified at the situation unfolding.

Even in the middle of it all, I remember noticing how small he looked—barefoot, bleary-eyed, confused.

I thought about Austin and Stephen. They were a team, thick as thieves, and I was the one who floated just outside their bubble. I'd referee, step in when they got too wild, roll my eyes when they made dumb jokes at dinner. Sometimes I envied their closeness. Sometimes I just wanted quiet. But I always loved them fiercely, in a way that felt almost like responsibility and almost like pride.

Now, our house was silent. It felt empty without my parents—without Austinand-Stephen making trouble.

A neighbor came over to stay with us. None of us had anything to say.

Austin and I sat on the couch together all night. Austin cried, and I held him.

In the midst of the terror, what I remember is Austin's tears. He and Stephen were always fighting, always tricking each other, always tattling. But that night, when facing a reality where Stephen might be gone, I saw how much they really loved each other too.

——————

My Dad came home in the early hours of the morning. He brought news, but not enough. Stephen was alive and stable. Stephen had a grand mal seizure—one that affects the whole brain. Most grand mal seizures last two minutes and stop on their own, but Stephen's went on for hours. The local hospital couldn't stop it. They called Flight for Life. A helicopter transported him to the nearest Children's Hospital. There, the doctors finally made it stop. Stephen and my mom were there now. Stephen was alive. He seemed to be okay, but there was still a lot we didn't know.

"Lauren, we need you to drive," my dad said. "I'll take one car, and you can take the other. We need to leave a car at the hospital so your mom can get home."

I'd only had my license for two weeks, and I had never driven on the highway alone. My stomach churned at the thought of the road ahead. But I knew I could do it.

——————

I parked the car. We were at the hospital. I opened the door and stepped out.

"You made it," my dad said.

I nodded.

Austin came over and grabbed my hand. We walked into the hospital, and up to the room my mom and Stephen were in. Stephen was laying on the bed, fast asleep. He had an IV running through his arm. He seemed tiny in that bed. Fragile.

My dad walked over to my mom and gave her a hug. Austin and I followed. We wrapped our arms around her.

Then, we all turned to look at Stephen.

"He's going to be okay," my mom said. "It's going to be a lot of work, but he's going to be okay."

——————

When I look back at that day—one that continues to be one of the scariest of my life—I think about both the powerlessness I felt, and the love I witnessed in my family. I couldn't stop the seizure. I couldn't make the ambulance go faster. But I could dial the number. I could drive the car. I could hold my brother's hand, hug my mom and dad, and hold my family close.

That night didn't make us perfect siblings. It didn't erase the teasing or the arguments. But it reminded me that when everything is on the line—when it really mattered—we show up for each other. And to me, that's what family really is—not constant harmony but knowing who will be there when the world goes silent.

Memoirs, Narratives, Poetry, and Spoken-Word Performances

Acevedo, Elizabeth. *Hair*. The George Washington University, 2015. https://www.youtube.com/watch?v=0I11xCfnzXs.

Acevedo, Elizabeth. *The Poet X*. New York: HarperTeen, an imprint of HarperCollins Publishers, 2020.

Alsaid, Adi, ed. *Come on In: 15 Stories About Immigration and Finding Home*. Toronto: Inkyard Press, 2021.

Bechdel, Alison. *Fun Home: A Family Tragicomic*. Boston: Houghton Mifflin Company: A Mariner book, 2007.

Bell, Cece. *El Deafo*. Superpowered edition. New York: Amulet Books, 2020.

Bell, Cece. *El Deafo—a Note from the Author*. YouTube. Apple TV+, 2022. https://www.youtube.com/watch?v=DnpGDjfyTiM&t=1s

Bryant, Kobe. *Dear Basketball—Kobe Bryant (1978–2020)*. Nikos Elite, 2020. https://www.youtube.com/watch?v=lUcdx4W8Xes.

Cisneros, Sandra. *The House on Mango Street*. 2nd ed. New York: Knopf Doubleday Publishing Group, 2013.

Cisneros, Sandra. *Woman Hollering Creek: And Other Stories*. Vintage Contemporaries Series. New York: Knopf Doubleday Publishing Group, 2013.

Dicks, Matt. "Gummi Bears Forever | *The Moth* (En-US) | Stories." *The Moth*, April 2, 2025. https://themoth.org/stories/gummi-bears-forever.

Doyle, Glennon. *Untamed*. New York: The Dial Press, 2020.

Fletcher, Ralph J. *Marshfield Dreams: When I Was a Kid*. New York: Square Fish, 2012.

Flett, Julie. *Birdsong*. Vancouver; Berkeley, CA: Greystone Kids, 2019.

Gharib, Malaka. *I Was Their American Dream: A Graphic Memoir*. New York: Clarkson Potter Publishers, 2019.

Green, John. "Googling Strangers and Kentucky Bluegrass | The Anthropocene Reviewed." WNYC Studios. March 28, 2018. https://www.wnycstudios.org/podcasts/anthropocene-reviewed/episodes/episode-3-googling-strangers-and-kentucky-bluegrass.

Green, John. *The Anthropocene Reviewed: Essays on a Human-Centered Planet*. Signed edition. New York: Dutton, 2021.

Hart, Tom. *Rosalie Lightning*. New York: St. Martin's Press, 2016.

King, Stephen. *Billy Summers*. New York: Scribner, 2021.

Lacayo, Alfonso. *The Moth* Presents Alfonso Lacayo: "The Bad Haircut." *The Moth*, 2015. https://www.youtube.com/watch?v=lLNTSjlZ0z8.

Lyon, George Ella. "Where I'm From." *Where I'm From Project* (blog), 1993. http://www.georgeellalyon.com/where.html.

Mahmoud, Emi. *Individual World Poetry Slam Finals 2015—Emi Mahmoud Final Round*, 2016. https://www.youtube.com/watch?v=IspMMNR8EOo.

Morales, Areli, illustrated by Luisa Uribe. *Areli Is a Dreamer: A True Story by Areli Morales, a DACA Recipient*. New York: Random House Studio, 2021.

Noah, Trevor. *It's Trevor Noah: Born a Crime: Stories from a South African Childhood, Adapted for Young Readers*. New York: Yearling, 2020.

Nye, Naomi Shihab. *Honeybee: Poems & Short Prose*. New York: Greenwillow Books, 2008.

Phi, Bao, and Thi Bui (Illustrator). *A Different Pond*. North Mankato, MN: Picture Window Books, 2017.

Quintero, Isabel, illustrated by Zeke Peña. *My Papi Has a Motorcycle*. New York: Kokila, an imprint of Penguin Books, 2019.

Satrapi, Marjane. *Persepolis: The Story of a Childhood*. Translated by Mattias Ripa and Blake Ferris. New York: Pantheon Books, 2003.

Sedaris, David. *Me Talk Pretty One Day*. New York: Back Bay Books/Little, Brown & Co./Hachette Book Group, 2009.

Takei, George, Justin Eisinger, Steven Scott, Harmony Becker, and Gilberto Lazcano. *They Called Us Enemy*. Marietta, GA: Top Shelf Productions, an imprint of IDW Publishing, 2019.

Thomas, Angie. *The Hate U Give*. New York: Harper Collins Publishers, 2017.

Wang, Andrea, illustrated by Jason Chin. *Watercress*. New York: Holiday House, 2021.

Watson, Renée. "Black Like Me." *Rethinking Schools*, Fall 1995. https://rethinkingschools.org/articles/black-like-me/.

Watson, Renée. "This Body." In *Watch Us Rise* by Renée Watson and Ellen Hagan. New York: Bloomsbury Publishing, 2019. https://www.youtube.com/watch?v=F4D9Xg5COD4.

Westover, Tara. *Educated: A Memoir*. New York: Random House, 2018.

Woodson, Jacqueline. *Brown Girl Dreaming*. New York: Nancy Paulsen Books, an imprint of Penguin Group, 2014.

References

Ahmed, Sara K. *Being the Change: Lessons and Strategies to Teach Social Comprehension*. Portsmouth, NH: Heinemann, 2018.

Anderson, Jeff, Travis Leech, and Holly Durham. *Patterns of Power: Teaching Grammar Through Reading and Writing, Grades 9–12*. Portsmouth, NH: Stenhouse Publishers, 2022.

Baker-Bell, April. *Linguistic Justice: Black Language, Literacy, Identity, and Pedagogy*. New York: Routledge, 2020.

Bliss, Laura, David Dudley, Sarah Holder, Geoff Manaugh, Jessica Lee Martin, Angely Mercado, Taien Ng-Chan, et al., eds. *The Quarantine Atlas: Mapping Global Life Under COVID-19*. New York: Black Dog & Levanthal Publishers, an imprint of Perseus Books, LLC, a subsidiary of Hachette Book Group, Inc., 2022.

Bomer, Katherine. *Writing a Life: Teaching Memoir to Sharpen Insight, Shape Meaning—and Triumph over Tests*. Portsmouth, NH: Heinemann, 2005.

Chavez, Felicia Rose. *The Anti-Racist Writing Workshop: How to Decolonize the Creative Classroom*. Chicago: Haymarket Books, 2021.

Clark, Roy Peter. "How to Love Revision." Teachers College, Columbia University, January 10, 2012.

Clark, Roy Peter. *Writing Tools: 55 Essential Strategies for Every Writer*. Revised Little, Brown paperback edition, 10th anniversary edition. New York: Little, Brown and Company, 2016.

Cruz, Maria Colleen. *The Unstoppable Writing Teacher: Real Strategies for the Real Classroom*. Portsmouth, NH: Heinemann, 2015.

Damour, Lisa. *Under Pressure: Confronting the Epidemic of Stress and Anxiety in Girls*. New York: Random House Publishing Group, 2019.

Ehrenworth, Mary. *Vocabulary Connections: A Structured Approach to Deepening Students' Academic and Expressive Language*. New York: Routledge, 2025.

Ehrenworth, Mary, and Philip Seyfried. *AI-Enhanced Literacy: Practical Steps for Deepening Reading and Writing Instruction*. New York: Routledge, 2025.

Ehrenworth, Mary, and Vicki Vinton. *The Power of Grammar: Unconventional Approaches to the Conventions of Language*. Portsmouth, NH: Heinemann, 2005.

España, Carla. *Narrative Writing with Latinx Teens: Testimonios, Texts, and Teaching*. Oxford, UK: Taylor & Francis Group, 2024.

España, Carla, and Luz Yadira Herrera. *En Comunidad: Lessons for Centering the Voices and Experiences of Bilingual Latinx Students*. Portsmouth, NH: Heinemann, 2020.

Feldman, Joe. *Grading for Equity: What It Is, Why It Matters, and How It Can Transform Schools and Classrooms*. Second edition. Thousand Oaks, CA: Corwin Press, 2024.

Ferlazzo, Larry. "Gholdy Muhammad Champions 'Unearthing Joy' in Her New Book." *Education Week*, February 1, 2023, sec. Teaching & Learning, Teaching. https://www.edweek.org/teaching-learning/opinion-gholdy-muhammad-champions-unearthing-joy-in-her-new-book/2023/02.

Frey, Nancy, John Hattie, and Douglas Fisher. *Developing Assessment-Capable Visible Learners, Grades K–12: Maximizing Skill, Will, and Thrill*. Thousand Oaks, CA: Corwin Literacy, 2018.

García, Ofelia, and Tatyana Kleyn. *Translanguaging with Multilingual Students: Learning from Classroom Moments*. New York: Routledge, 2016.

García, Ofelia, Susana Ibarra Johnson, Kate Seltzer, and Guadalupe Valdés. *The Translanguaging Classroom: Leveraging Student Bilingualism for Learning*. Philadelphia: Caslon, 2017.

Guskey, Thomas. "Making High School Grades Meaningful." *Phi Delta Kappan* 87, no. 9 (2006): 670–675.

Guskey, Thomas R., Nancy Frey, and Douglas Fisher. *Grading with Integrity: A Research-Based Approach Grounded in Honesty, Transparency, Accuracy, and Equity*. Thousand Oaks, CA: Corwin, 2024.

Hammond, Zaretta. *Culturally Responsive Teaching and The Brain: Promoting Authentic Engagement and Rigor among Culturally and Linguistically Diverse Students*. Thousand Oaks, CA: Corwin, 2015.

Hattie, John, Douglas Fisher, Nancy Frey, and Shirley Clarke. *Collective Student Efficacy: Developing Independent and Inter-Dependent Learners*. Corwin Teaching Essentials, vol 1. Thousand Oaks, CA: Corwin, 2021.

Hattie, John. *Visible Learning, the Sequel: A Synthesis of over 2,100 Meta-Analyses Relating to Achievement*. London; New York: Routledge, 2023. https://doi.org/10.4324/9781003380542.

Howard, Tyrone, Tanya Milner-McCall, and Jaleel R. Howard. *No More Teaching Without Positive Relationships*. Portsmouth, NH: Heinemann, 2020.

Jason Reynolds National Ambassador for Young People's Literature, 2020. https://www.youtube.com/watch?v=qSos56YM6BM.

Jason Reynolds on Storytelling: Building Deeper Connections Through Stories, 2024. https://www.youtube.com/watch?v=_LLG2hcudxs.

Johnston, Howard. "Best Practices in Grading. Research into Practice." *Education Partnerships, Inc.* Education Partnerships, Inc, December 2011. https://eric.ed.gov/?id=ED538743.

Karr, Mary. *The Art of Memoir*. New York: Harper Perennial, 2016.

King, Stephen. *On Writing: A Memoir of the Craft*. New York: Scribner, 2010.

Kittle, Penny. *Write Beside Them: Risk, Voice, and Clarity in High School Writing*. Portsmouth, NH: Heinemann, 2008.

Lamott, Anne. *Bird by Bird: Some Instructions on Writing and Life*. Second Anchor Books edition. New York: Anchor Books, a division of Penguin Random House LLC, 2019.

Lyiscott, Jamila. Jamila Lyiscott: "3 Ways to Speak English." TED, 2014. https://www.youtube.com/watch?v=k9fmJ5xQ_mc.

Mollick, Ethan. *Co-Intelligence: Living and Working with AI.* New York: Penguin Random House LLC, 2024.

Muhammad, Gholdy. *Unearthing Joy: A Guide to Culturally and Historically Responsive Teaching and Learning.* New York: Scholastic Inc., 2023.

Pecheone, Ray, and Columbia University TCRWP. "Think Tank on Performance Assessments." Teachers College, Columbia University, October 2015.

Peña, Matt de la. "A Conversation with Matt de La Peña." Presented at *From Theory to Practice*, a Symposium with Advancing Literacy, Teachers College, Columbia University, October 3, 2023.

Reeves, Douglas B. "The Case Against the Zero." *Phi Delta Kappan* 86, no. 4 (December 1, 2004): 324–325. https://doi.org/10.1177/003172170408600418.

Ritchhart, Ron, Mark Church, and Karin Morrison. *Making Thinking Visible: How to Promote Engagement, Understanding, and Independence for All Learners.* San Francisco: Jossey-Bass, 2011.

Schnall, Marianne. "Interview with Isabel Allende." Feminist.com, July 11, 2008. https://www.feminist.com/resources/artspeech/interviews/isabelallende.html.

Truss, Lynne. *Eats, Shoots & Leaves: The Zero Tolerance Approach to Punctuation.* New York: Gotham Books, 2006.

Warner, John. *More Than Words: How to Think About Writing in the Age of AI.* New York: Basic Books, 2025.

Wiggins, Grant, and Jay McTighe. "Put Understanding First." ASCD, May 1, 2008. https://www.ascd.org/el/articles/put-understanding-first.

Wiggins, Grant P., and Jay McTighe. *Understanding by Design.* Expanded 2nd ed., Alexandria, VA: ASCD, 2024.

Wolf, Maryanne. *Reader, Come Home: The Reading Brain in a Digital World.* New York: Harper, an imprint of HarperCollinsPublishers, 2018.

Woodson, Jacqueline. "Keynote Address." Presented at the NJCTE Conference, March 20, 2025.

Acknowledgments

There are legions of writers and educators who have written memoir and taught memoir, and we are grateful to all of these mentors, including those who are intimate colleagues and those we admire from afar.

For instilling writing workshop and writing process in schools and inspiring generations of writing teachers, we honor the ground-breaking work of Don Murray, Don Graves, Lucy Calkins, Nancie Atwell, Penny Kittle, Ralph Fletcher, Linda Rief, Katie Wood Ray, and Katherine Bomer.

For deepening criticality, destabilizing oppressive power dynamics inside of writing workshop, and questioning how to make writing instruction more congenial for more learners, we especially honor Tom Newkirk, Felicia Rose Chavez, Ofelia García, Colleen Cruz, and Carla España.

For innovating grammar instruction and linguistic consciousness, we delight in the work of Jeff Anderson, Vicki Vinton, Roy Peter Clark, Jamila Lyiscott, and April Baker Bell—all writing teachers who love language, promote linguistic justice, and abhor rules.

For contributing to the thinking and the lessons in this book, we thank all of our colleagues whom we've collaborated with over the years through Teachers College, in particular, Kat Schechter and Angela Forero, with whom we coauthored earlier memoir units, and whose beautiful, critical, inclusive thinking informs these pages; and Phil Seyfreid, whose innovative thinking about AI helped shape all our AI lessons. We also thank our friends in high school classrooms, especially Jenny Killion and Lauren Freer at the American School of Barcelona; Christen Klewicki and Shehnaz Khalfan-Washington at Rye School District, New York; Sharon Larpenteur of Beaverton, Oregon; Robert Ciarrocca of Cranford High School, New Jersey; and the teachers and leaders at Columbia High School in Maplewood, New Jersey.

Finally, we are so grateful to the team at Stenhouse/Routledge. Not many large publishers can still feel like small teams, but this one does. Thank you to Melanie Moy and Hannah Sroka for help along the way with all our production questions, permissions requests, and countless emails. Thank you to Sam Meagher for offering your wisdom and expertise. Our book is better because your eyes were on it. Thank you to Pamela Hunt for copyediting so patiently. Thank you to Elizabeth Spicer for bringing the book to production.

And thank you most of all to our editor, Terry Thompson, for his patience, his coaching, his joy in writing and teaching. Terry is a bit of a legend as an education editor, and it's for a reason. Terry, you bring out the best in every writer and teacher, and the best in how we move through this world.

Index

For Product Safety Concerns and Information,
please contact our EU representative GPSR@taylorandfrancis.com
Taylor & Francis Verlag GmbH, Kaufingerstraße 24,
80331 München, Germany

Printed by Integrated Books International,
United States of America